M000234976

"The effect of reading this book warmth and intimacy here that presentations of theology. It's like to pull up a chair at the breakfast room table where two wise and gentle monks are having a conversation, pondering the deepest thoughts of their hearts. Their conversation draws on insights from the enduring religions of the world as well as from psychology, philosophy, and poetry. But it is all grounded in the real stuff of ordinary, human life. Brother David and Father Anselm delve deeply into places of the human heart that every reader knows well, and you might find yourself marvelling at how well they seem to know and embrace you. The words *conversation* and *conversion* share a common root—one conveys friendly intimacy and the other conveys dramatic power. This book conveys both."

> —The Reverend Gary D. Jones
> Rector of St. Stephen's Episcopal Church
> Richmond, Virginia

"What an inspiring book! I feel humbled and greatly enriched by discovering the pearls of wisdom revealed in these challenging conversations. We meet two spiritual masters speaking from the depths of their hearts and a wealth of experience. The deepest insights of spiritual life are presented here with so much discernment, beauty, and love as well as great simplicity. They open up the treasures of faith beyond all well-worn doctrines, rituals, and beliefs by concentrating on the heart of religion, its life-giving energies, and its eternal message of trust and hope. This book is a precious gift, a real treasure. Let us hope that it will be discovered by many people and give them a deep sense of trust, strength, and joy."

> —Ursula King
> University of Bristol, England

"This is an extraordinary conversation between two of the most eloquent voices in contemporary Benedictine monasticism. Br. David, whose poetic, prophetic rearticulation of ancient truths has inspired believers and nonbelievers across the globe, and Fr. Anselm, with his prodigious output of practical down-to-earth monastic spirituality, invite us into an intimate colloquy that at times is nothing short of breathtaking in its vision of and for Christianity."

> —Cyprian Consiglio, OSB Cam.
> Author of *Spirit, Soul, Body*

"*Faith beyond Belief* reawakens the ancient form of monastic writing known as a 'chapter': brief, condensed writing on a host of topics. Together these two revered, spiritual masters from the Benedictine tradition offer reflections and guidance on the deep-tissue, spiritual topics of our day. Their reflections shimmer with wisdom as they traverse the pathless path of prayer with poise and proclaim it in perfect pitch. Readers will find their gratitude expanding into canyons of receptive reverence for the wisdom and perspective that David Steindl-Rast and Anselm Grün, each in his own way, offer to each one of us."

> —Martin Laird
> Author of *Into the Silent Land* and *A Sunlit Absence*

"Readers are treated in *Faith beyond Belief* to a unique opportunity to be a 'fly on the wall' and listen in on a thought-provoking series of discussions between two of the greatest spiritual writers of our time. This volume presents a wide-ranging array of timely theological, spiritual, and cultural themes that will not leave those already familiar with David Steindl-Rast and Anselm Grün disappointed. Those new to their creative and original engagement with faith, tradition, and dialogue will surely find this a welcome entrée to their respective works."

> —Daniel P. Horan, OFM
> Catholic Theological Union
> Author of *The Franciscan Heart of Thomas Merton: A New Look at the Spiritual Inspiration of His Life, Thought, and Writing*

"*Faith beyond Belief* presents a compelling blend of scholarly and practical insights, grounded in ancient traditions and texts while also providing fresh approaches to meaning-making in a diverse and global society. The wide-ranging dialogue explores the basic values found at the heart of all religions—gratitude, courage, self-knowledge, forgiveness, compassion—each one oriented toward sustaining positive human relationships. The authors excel at illuminating nuances when they encounter points of tension—from exploring the hidden value of suffering, to reconciling the goals of self-acceptance and self-mastery, to navigating religious and nonreligious approaches to social justice and environmental crises. The result is an impassioned and inspirational book that calls for each of us—no matter our belief system—to connect with the heart of what it means to be human. And furthermore, it points to practical steps toward this noble aim."

> —Geshe Lobsang Tenzin Negi, PhD
> Director of the Emory-Tibet Partnership at Emory University

# Faith beyond Belief

*Spirituality for Our Times*

## A Conversation

David Steindl-Rast and Anselm Grün

*Edited by*
Johannes Kaup

*Translated by*
Linda M. Maloney

*Foreword by*
Martin E. Marty

**LITURGICAL PRESS**
Collegeville, Minnesota

www.litpress.org

Cover design by Ann Blattner. Cover photo: Father Anselm Grün and Brother David Steindl-Rast in conversation at the Abbey of Münsterschwarzach. © Johannes Kaup / Vier-Türme-Verlag.

This work was originally published in German as *Das Glauben Wir.* Copyright © 2015 by Vier Türme GmbH-Verlag, Münsterschwarzach.

| 1 | 2 | 3 | 4 | 5 | 6 | 7 | 8 | 9 |
|---|---|---|---|---|---|---|---|---|

**Library of Congress Cataloging-in-Publication Data**

Names: Grün, Anselm, author. | Steindl-Rast, David, author.
Title: Faith beyond belief : spirituality for our times : a conversation / David Steindl-Rast and Anselm Grün ; edited by Johannes Kaup ; translated by Linda M. Maloney.
Other titles: Glauben Wir. English
Description: Collegeville, Minnesota : Liturgical Press, 2016. | Includes bibliographical references.
Identifiers: LCCN 2016007165 (print) | LCCN 2016015434 (ebook) | ISBN 9780814647134 (pbk.) | ISBN 9780814647387 (ebook)
Subjects: LCSH: Spirituality—Christianity. | Theology.
Classification: LCC BV4501.3 .G79513 2016 (print) | LCC BV4501.3 (ebook) | DDC 248—dc23
LC record available at https://lccn.loc.gov/2016007165

# Contents

# Foreword

*"Discovery is our business."* Quite naturally, most scientists would define their searches in such terms. One of them, a Nobel Prize–winning scientist, is often pictured with the original motto, in Chinese, framed above his desk. Now, thanks to the generosity of a family member of its original owner, it hangs behind my shoulder as I, a nonscientist, go about my work. Of course, the calligraphic announcement invites questions, as it is supposed to. What does that saying have to do with studies in the humanities, in my case, of history and theology? "I'm glad you asked that." As we read ancient sacred texts we are not being antiquarians. We hope to discover meanings appropriate to our times, our searches.

"Discovery is our business" serves well to describe the vocations and intentions of Anselm Grün and David Steindl-Rast. They are seeking deeper meanings than those that are readily available on superficial levels, meanings that may seem hidden or obscure but that they both know and show can now be of as much help to us readers as they were in their own moments of discovery.

"Discovery is our business." How do the two authors go about their business in this case? Through conversation, dutifully recorded, transcribed, edited, and published. Sages and scholars can impart knowledge by spelling out doctrines or imposing dicta, because they know some answers, can argue for them, and helpfully expound them. If argument is governed by a person's knowing answers, conversation is guided by posing questions, in familiar give-and-take or take-and-give exchanges.

"Discovery is our business." What is our role in this exploration? Since the two authors are conversing with each other, we might at first think of ourselves as being mere overhearers, intentional eavesdroppers, or ill-mannered kibitzers. If we are ill-at-ease in such roles, Anselm and David—we can call them that here—minister to us reassuringly by what they say and how they say it. Some conversations exclude others, but in this book they are inclusive, open, inviting. That is clear from the way Anselm and David set out to inform or persuade each other, by confessing their own limits, describing their experiences and experiments on their path to discovery.

Conversation that we hear on these pages is anything but chatter on the level we expect among most tweeters and twitterers. Did I say we "hear" the conversation? It is easy to forget that we are reading, so realistic and vivid are the contributions from both Anselm and David. And it is clear that both speakers are veteran communicators to various kinds of individuals, audiences, and publics. They never forget the single "other" hearer in their two-way communications, but they draw on so many levels of discovery that we can tell they are writing for "others," for all of us.

To win us and hold us, they have to have something to say that matches what we seek to discover. Far from casually chattering, they demonstrate their at-homeness with mystics, prophets, and scholars with whom they are familiar and whom they would like us to know better. The endnotes confirm what page-by-page readers will have discovered: the names of titans and giants who help shape the spiritual search through the ages and especially in our epoch appear on page after page. But just as this conversation is not chatter, so the citations are not here because the two authors are name-droppers. No, they have listened to, learned from, or read diverse sources from Bavarian Catholicism to the Tibet of the Dalai Lama or the Japan of Buddhists.

Since this is not intended to be a reference work, it will at times appear to be haphazardly organized; one of the authors admits this. Go elsewhere, one is advised, if you want a formal catechism or encyclopedia. Not that the authors are opposed to such literature. It is simply not their vocation, in this setting, to work with formulas and formal schemes. As I was reading this, I pictured painterly analogies, most vividly to the genre of impressionists like Claude Monet. Where in it are the figurative right angles, straight lines, and formalities that serve dogmaticians, systematic theologians, and lexicographers so well? The first glance in most chapters here is blurry, subtle. Yet whoever has stood before the works of impressionist art in great galleries, and there has given himself or herself to the artists, is likely to have formed memorable impressions of gardens and gateways, water lilies and windows. From these, viewers and ponderers are likely to have found that they have discovered something unforgettable or at least less forgettable. They will remember the images as they become clarified in fresh ways.

Tempted as I am to exegete or expound some of the probings and depictions left by Anselm and David, I have learned from the way they go about things to keep disquisitions brief—and then get out of the way. That leaves the scene open for them as they help us about our business: spiritual discovery.

Martin E. Marty

# Prologue

## Erg Chebbi, Morocco

Here I am at last. High up, on the biggest sand dune for miles around. The Algerian border is a mile or two behind me. In the far distance, the red-gold ball of fire is sinking behind a table mountain. The first stars are twinkling in the firmament. Our dusty motorcycles and igloo-shaped tents stand at the foot of these mountains of sand; from up here I can scarcely make them out. My friends stayed below, searching out dry roots and dung for the evening's fire. The three blue-robed Bedouins on camels disappeared hours ago into a valley between the dunes. My lips are dry. I let the fine, cool sand run through my fingers like water. Desert wherever I turn my eyes. Not a breath of wind. Not a sound. Silence over the earth. Silence in heaven. Silence within me. I breathe in. I breathe out. I am here. Entirely here. Now! In this moment, it is as if scales fall from my eyes: I have arrived at the center of the universe. Then I remember all the places in which that was true: Scotland, Norway, Mongolia, New Mexico . . .

But the geography is a minor detail. Ultimately, it is not about special places. When one is traveling—and in some sense we are journeying throughout our lives—it is about moments in which the passage of time seems suddenly arrested. Everything I think I have to be and do, everything I am seeking and even the things in which I have failed—all that falls away in such moments. I feel altogether naked. But I am. Entirely. Here. As if from nothing, the silence within me begins to speak, softly, inaudibly.

People appear around me, the living and those long dead. Encounters that have shaped me come to life. Joyful and painful, delightful and disappointing—everything is transparent to this single moment. There is no more separation between me and the world, between my ego and my Self, between my history and that of others, between being and time. Everything is altogether clear. The goal of the journey is within my grasp. It is in such moments that I am completely flooded with love. If I had to die then, I would be ready. Nothing but concern for my loved ones would hold me back.

Sometimes the conversation becomes a silent song. It sings itself within me. Just so. Pure happiness. What better meaning could there be for my life than to respond in gratitude for the gift of being. Through, with, and for others. Thankful for the invisible sources whose origins reach back into nothingness . . . here in the middle of the Moroccan desert and everywhere I am and will be.

What does all that have to do with this book? Some will already guess; I ask that others be patient for a few more lines. First, a change of place.

This summer is peculiar: cool, wet, and windy. To the west, above the Burgundian hills, another dark line of clouds moves over the little village. Here, seventy-five years ago, Brother Roger Schütz, from Switzerland, came to found a monastery that would be a symbol of reconciliation in a world wounded by divisions. A life of simplicity in the spirit of the Gospel of Jesus and companionship with people of today. Since the 1960s that community at the edge of the little village has been a meeting place for thousands of young people from all over the world. Such thousands gather several times a day for the regular prayer times, the mantra-like singing, times of silence, and times of dialogue in the long, candlelit nave of the church. They come from all over Europe: Sweden, Germany, and Spain, Ireland, Italy, and Ukraine. There are a few guests from South Korea, the Philippines, Nigeria, Brazil, Argentina. They sit and kneel, close packed, praying, singing, keeping silence. This assembly is not a classic audience. You can sense that for some it is a "first" in their lives.

The different languages, cultures, mentalities, and ways of life shape the temporary community of thousands into an image of the global village in which we live virtually nowadays. And yet with a major difference: Here we look into each other's eyes, listen to each other, share simple meals, clean the showers and toilets together, read Bible texts together and share our life experiences with one another. We are varied and different, and yet we are one. Not because we know so much, but because we are seeking, open, present in the spirit of newcomers. Here it does not matter what you have but only who you are. Simplicity in the multiplicity of forms. Unity that does not iron out differences or suppress them. This is a fundamental unity that allows individual uniqueness to be, that enables and rejoices in the cultural choir of voices and splendor of colors that enriches the world here. An anticipation of the utopia of a new Europe and of global common life—here it has a place and can be experienced as reality.

My glance wanders slowly through the dimly lit church. Here young people are gathered, hungry for a spirituality for our time. Will they discover the hidden treasures that have repeatedly given new life to Christianity? Will they find credible witnesses who can translate the core message of Jesus Christ in an authentic way for today? Will they be able to live a mysticism that turns toward the world, that reveals itself as practical politics in its care for and solidarity with the world's outsiders? Will they become agents of a transformation to a global commonality that our world so urgently needs?

For me, Brother David Steindl-Rast and Father Anselm Grün are such figures of hope, people who by the power of their example can offer an orientation in a world that has become too complex to comprehend. Knowing them and spending a whole weekend with them in the monastery of Münsterschwarzach, leading deep, vital exchanges, has filled me with great joy and gratitude. The spirituality they radiate is an everyday thing that is nevertheless both profound and vivid. Their life experiences, their gift for critical spiritual discernment, their radical honesty, their considered, poetic language, their therapeutic-spiritual knowledge, and their capacity for humor and self-directed irony have inspired and delighted me for many years.

In fact, the impulse for our conversations came from Pope Francis's native land: Alberto Rizzo from Buenos Aires conceived the idea and persuaded Brother David Steindl-Rast to participate. All that remained for me was to consult with Anselm Grün to see whether it would be possible to find a common time slot in the close-packed appointment calendars of the two spiritual masters. When that was accomplished, and we met together in Münsterschwarzach, the Spirit was free to flow.

Our conversations, now in book form, could be read as a "crash course" in Christian spirituality. Because of the conversational form and the limited time available to us, some readers may well miss one or another topic and find that the chapters are not organized systematically. I am to blame for that. But I think this book will be an inspiration and an aid to spiritual life for many people of our time, whether they are believers or not. In this sense I, as a radio journalist, hope I can count on the "vocal journalism" of those who are touched and enlightened by it.

Johannes Kaup
Erg Chebbi, Taizé, and Vienna
November 2014

# First Love, or:

## *Childhood Sources of Solidarity*

*What people believe, how they understand and live their spirituality, is influenced above all by their childhood experiences. Therefore, reflection on spirituality is always also a search for traces, a reflection on our first profound experiences of the Holy, with what the world's religions describe as the divine.*

### David Steindl-Rast

My earliest memory of an experience of the Holy goes way back—I must have been about four years old. It was just before Christmas, and there was a gold thread from Christmas wrapping on the floor of my parents' bedroom. I asked excitedly what it was, and my mother said: "It must be a hair from the Christ Child." That moved me deeply. It was not silly then, and it is not silly as I remember it today. The experience both drew me and made me shudder—that is, it was a true encounter with the Holy.

You could object that such an experience is soon demythologized when one grows older. But for me the transition from Christ Child to a broader outlook was quite easy because my parents were very skillful. They simply said: "The Christ Child sent us." That Christ lives in everyone and everything and that he loves in us was something I could easily translate.

Another memory: I was still very small, at most five, when I saw an airplane writing "IMI" in the sky with steam or white gas of some kind. It was an advertisement for a cleaning product. The plane was tiny—I couldn't even recognize it as a plane—so it must have been flying very high. So I asked: "What is that?" and the answer was: "That is the skywriter." (Planes like that were called "skywriters" back then.) I immediately thought of the Holy Spirit because the plane really did look like a tiny dove writing on the sky. That was, for me, another encounter—a real one—with the Holy.

A third incident I remember, perhaps one or two years later, was a dream: Our house had a circular stone staircase from the ground floor (where we children and our parents lived) to the second floor (where my grandmother and great-grandmother lived). I always called it the "old floor." In my dream I was going down the circular staircase, and Jesus was coming up it. He looked like the picture in my grandmother's room. When we met, we merged into one another. That was the dream. Nothing more. I didn't think about the dream for decades, but I could never forget it. I now understand it as a true spiritual experience.

In themselves these early experiences were perhaps not so very important, but all these childhood encounters with the Holy that I remember have to do with Christian teaching. From the beginning, the spiritual was for me entirely embedded in the Christian form of its expression and in Christian ritual.

Interestingly, Nature did not move me as deeply as religious things. We were in the mountains quite often, because my mother was a great mountaineer; we always looked wonderingly up at mountain peaks and cliffs and said: "Mama was up there!" But experiences of Nature were not really peak experiences, except for this one: Opposite the one little store in our village, behind some fruit trees, was a hidden spring that bubbled out through a little wooden pipe. While my mother was shopping I liked to sit alone and in silence by that spring in the orchard. And the miracle that fresh water came out from deep in the earth was also a true peak experience—in the encounter with Nature, without any explicit thought of God.

### Anselm Grün

For me, too, the mysterious was first sensed at Christmas. We children waited upstairs until the bell rang and we went down. The living room was full of candles—that was already a kind of mystery, a shivery thing. Other such experiences were strongly linked to the liturgy. I well remember that I took my first communion very seriously. Becoming one with Christ—that was a spiritual experience. And the Holy Week liturgy when I was eight or nine years old—and later as an altar server—that was something holy. At such times I experienced something numinous and, therefore, when I was only ten years old, I told my father that I was thinking of becoming a priest. Of course, that was still a childish idea. But I do remember that I experienced a special fascination with liturgy and its mysteries at my first communion, which I took very, very seriously.

Later I sensed particular experiences in Nature as encounters with the Holy. Once I was in the woods and heard a noise: the rushing wind was like a union with God and with all things. That was a very profound experience.

My father, who went for a walk with me and my siblings every Sunday, always pointed out the beauty of Nature to us: the trees, the birds, the starry sky. In that sense Nature was always something important. The mountains, in particular, were the grandest and most majestic things for us children. When evening came and the sun set behind high mountains, I sensed the Holy. Then I was very still and simply looked. But for me the liturgy was the beginning.

# A God beyond the Marketplace, or:

## Who Is God, Now That God Is "Dead"?

*Many people nowadays find that their daily lives are ruled by powers and forces that seem to have nothing to do with faith and religion. In industrialized societies the lives of many are shaped primarily by work, and they have very little control over their working conditions. The market determines what is good, important, and worth working for. Government tries—more or less successfully—to smooth out life's risks with social safety nets, at least in the "welfare states." It's all about achievement, competition, and success. In poor countries, most people's lives are focused on the daily struggle to stay alive. In the emerging countries there is a growing global consumer class modeled on Western lifestyles. In contrast to the majority who are still poor and "impoverished," this new class is interested in and oriented toward material growth above all things. In all these phenomena there seems to be no room for God, who has in some sense become superfluous, a faded thing from a murky time of insecurity that at most is believed in by the "ignorant" as their last consolation. Is God dead, as the German philosopher Friedrich Nietzsche[1] thought when he said "we have killed him"?*

### Anselm Grün

For many people, God is not the primal reality; God is not an obvious fact. But in the world's wealthy societies especially, there are many who sense that money and the struggle for survival cannot be all there is. I constantly experience their longing for more: to be loved, to be accepted unconditionally, a desire to feel that a greater mystery surrounds us. People ask me: Where can I get the strength to continue the struggle? Is there nothing but what we see around us, or is there another dimension? I get these questions from poor people and from those who have made money. Least approachable are the newly rich who think they have everything and need to put their wealth on display. When people suppress their longing, they find themselves empty and hollow. But I personally believe that all the rest sense their longing. I agree with St. Augustine,[2] who said that when someone fights passionately and desires—whether love or success or money and riches—there is always something more behind it, ultimately a longing for God.

### David Steindl-Rast

I understand humans, as humans, to be the "religious animals." Among all the animals, we are the ones who are oriented toward the *mysterium*, who always seek to go beyond ourselves. How consciously we do that depends on a number of things. Those who are totally absorbed in the struggle for survival have no time for it, and those who are pursuing success have no interest in it. But all people are existentially oriented toward the Great Mystery of being. Sooner or later—when we experience the death of a good friend, when we fail, when we are confronted with illness and perhaps with our own death—questions arise, fundamental questions about our relationship to that Mystery, the Mystery of the divine. "God" originally meant "the one called upon." The word "God" is therefore not a name; it points to our existential orientation to the Mystery.

Every person will be confronted sooner or later with transcendence, with a reality that is infinitely beyond us, by way of three questions:

The first question is: "Why?" Everyone asks, sooner or later, "Why?" Why do I even exist? Why is there something and not nothing? Why can I ask: "Why?" This leads us inevitably into the divine Mystery.

The second question is: "What?" We ask ourselves: What is the ultimate reality? What is this or that in its innermost being? "What," unlike the vertical plane of "why," lies on the horizontal plane, to put it in visual terms. "Why" draws us into unfathomable depths, "what" into the remotest distances. On this level there is always more and more. So Goethe says, "If you want to reach the infinite, explore the finite in every direction."[3] The infinite "what" leads us into the same mystery as the unfathomable "why."

And the third question is: How? Here we stand, so to speak, at the axis of deep and wide, and ask "how." Ultimately that means: How should I live? How do I manage it? How do I do it? This makes the whole process dynamic. We stumble upon the *mysterium* in the inexhaustible dynamic of being itself.

I think that asking these three questions is something altogether human. Cultural forms can be very different, but it is an existential element of humanity. In Christian language we call this Mystery "God," and the three questions point to the Trinity, for "why" leads us into the depth of the divine Mystery, what we as Christians call "Father," while "what" draws us into the breadth of the "cosmic Christ," and "how" brings us into the dynamic of the "Holy Spirit."

## Anselm Grün

For me personally it is a very different question that ultimately leads me into the mystery of God, namely, "Who am I?
Am I a man, a woman, this one or that one? Am I a priest or
a father, a mother or wife of . . . ?" When I probe deeper and
deeper, I also arrive at a mystery. Recently, also, the subject of
beauty—in art, in Nature, but also in music, painting, poetry,
the beauties of language—all that has become important to
me. Why do people long for beauty? Plato[4] says that everything that exists is beautiful, true, and good. God is "beauty
itself." If I follow that thread to its end I discover that even
poor people have a sense of beauty, just like everyone else.

Simone Weil,[5] who was herself very poor and worked
on behalf of the poor, still needed beauty in order to live.
Dostoevsky[6] says: once a year you must look at the "Sistine
Madonna" in order to cope with the beauty in your life. That
is important to me, too, because it is a trace of God in the
world. When someone is fixated on money, the beautiful is
meaningless. Of course, anyone can fill up an apartment in
a completely tasteless way and be proud of it, but that has
nothing to do with beauty.

In the past I have seen spirituality primarily as an en-
counter with myself: trying to discern God's truth there.
That is one way. But beauty points to a different image of
God: the *fruitio Dei*—enjoying God, not just always obeying
God. God is the one who fascinates us, who gives us beauty.

Dostoevsky says, quite accurately: Beauty will save the
world. And Jesus implanted the idea of beauty in his disciples so that they might become brothers and sisters. So it's
not: "you have to love!" but "when I have a sense of the
beautiful in myself and in the other, we are brother and sister." That is not moralizing. Beauty leads to a belonging-to
and love for one another.

*I have to counter you—or beauty—with something else. Let me use Friedrich Nietzsche as an example. "God is dead! We have killed him!" Nietzsche thought that God as the "highest being" had become impossible. If I think of God in that way, as the supreme thing, seated high up on top of a pyramid and legitimating all the power structures in our world, we have a huge problem. God was misused in that way for many centuries. You yourself, in your youth, experienced the ideology of National Socialism, which was a consequence of the fact that we had "killed" God; then a Führer came to take God's place. In Communism the party filled the gap left by God. Today we might say it is the "free" market, the total market, that determines the conditions of our lives and the structures of commerce. An idol always takes the place of the Most High—when the place is unoccupied. But that is the experience we have when we do not pay attention to God among us, at our center: then—as Jesus would say—the house is always occupied by "demons" or idols that disorient and destroy our lives.*

### Anselm Grün

Nietzsche was quite right. He thought that a particular image of God was dead: the moralizing God, the God who always demands sacrifice, who is only denial; that God is dead. But Nietzsche also suffered from the fact.

For me, one thing is important: Nietzsche desired the beautiful, the Dionysian; he had a sense of it. There is a sentence in his papers that reads something like, "Where despair meets longing, there is mysticism." That is the leap into the Mystery. Nietzsche sensed despair, but longing as well. The two have to be held together. It is not a mysticism I can dream about, one I can possess, but a feeling, a sense—a leap into the Mystery.

## David Steindl-Rast

Ultimately, Nietzsche was a deeply religious man. The last verse of his poem, "The Unknown God," reads:

> I want to know You, Unknown One
> You, who have reached deep into my soul,
> into my life like the gust of a storm.
> You incomprehensible yet related one!
> I want to know you, even serve you.[7]

## Anselm Grün

After all, he was the son of a Lutheran pastor and struggled against the negative view of God and humanity he found in his father's religion. God and beauty were not at all connected there; God was the denial of life. Clearly, Nietzsche took the wrong path, and the Nazis misused his saying about the "higher man."[8] He certainly suffered, sensed something, and took it beyond all measure, but he is and remains a challenge for us.

# Where Are You Alive? or:

## The Creative Meaning of Life

*When people ask about the meaning and purpose of human life, they find a variety of answers. Some say that life itself is its own meaning. Others are primarily interested in the greatest possible realization of their personal potential. Still others prefer the constructivist variant: meaning is what we ourselves construct, shape, and realize in different contexts. But are these answers really satisfying, or are they just bewildering? It is worth inquiring more deeply about what makes humanity what it is and what moves human beings at the depth of their being. What answers do David Steindl-Rast and Anselm Grün have to offer to questions about the meaning and purpose of life as they survey decades of their own lives and the world's history?*

### David Steindl-Rast

As long as we try to grasp meaning—that is, "get a grip on it"—we are on the wrong track, because our grip is not big enough to grab onto meaning. Bernard of Clairvaux[9] says: "Instruction makes us learned. Affective experience makes us wise." Allowing oneself to be seized, to be moved, is to discover meaning. When we experience emotion, meaning is simply there. Such experience is a discovery of meaning. I think everyone undergoes this again and again, for example, when a child is born or when one is engulfed by the beauty of art or Nature. Many people experience the religious nowadays only in encounter with what is over-whelming in Nature.

Of course, one may also be seized by hatred and delusions. People shouted their frenetic "Yes!" when Joseph Goebbels, Hitler's chief of propaganda, harangued his party members in 1943, in the so-called "Sport Palace Speech" in Berlin: "Do you want total war?" Here we have to use a very sharp scalpel to separate the emotion that is positive in itself and the emotion that is exploited to wrong ends. As such, this exploited emotion in a large group is not so different from a situation in which one hears Beethoven's[10] Ninth Symphony and is moved by it, or the moment when one stands in the natural world, dumbfounded by a waterfall. Emotional experience is something positive, but it can be exploited.

For many people, life as such offers the most immediate access to the experience of God. Within life itself we experience the Great Mystery. Science can say a good deal about how a living being functions, but *what* life is—that is something no scientist can tell; nor is that the task of science. Philosophers cannot tell it either, and theologians can only point to the fact that it is possible for us to experience life as a divine mystery. At the same time, this indicates that the divine reality is not "out there." There is always a danger that we may think God is separated from us. When we speak of life as a divine mystery, it is evident that we are fully immersed in God, and God in us, because we cannot say whether *we* have life or life has *us*.

People are differently ready for the God question at different times. In childhood we are open to it, but then there comes a time when we have very different questions in our minds. I think we have made the mistake of supposing that catechesis is possible at any age. But in life there are times for catechesis and times when we have to say: wait a while.

Still, even if people do not think much about God during certain phases of their lives, those are still important times to experience God. Later we will reflect on them. But I think we need to give people time. If you are not ready to reflect on God and your experience of the ultimate reality, then wait.

### Anselm Grün

When somebody asks me about meaning, I like to give three answers. One: meaning is that I let this unique image God has made of me become visible in my life. All my life long, I am on the way, seeking this unique image, the answer to this question of "who am I?" and trying to live authentically. Then my life has meaning.

Second, there is the question of my mission. Jesus sends people. What is my calling? It need not be anything special, but still, I am not here simply to feel good. I have a mission, a duty in the world.

Third, I refer to Viktor Frankl,[11] who thought a lot about meaning. First, he speaks of "creative meaning": When I do something creative, it is meaningful. Then there is experienced meaning: when I experience something profound and am seized by it, I ask about its meaning. Then it is meaningful. Finally, there is the meaning that lies in our attitudes, the values we apply. For example, the death of a child is meaningless in itself, but the important thing is how I react to it. Frankl says that fate can take everything from you, even your life, but one thing it cannot take away: your freedom to respond and to give even hard things a meaning. We have within us the "defiant power of the spirit" that can derive meaning even from illness. It is not that illness is meaningful, but I can give it a meaning.

There are also people who bemoan that things are going badly for them, and they find no meaning in life. Then I ask: What moves you? I am sometimes shocked when they say: "Nothing." There is nothing, not music, not art, not poetry, not Nature. There are even some who are no longer moved and drawn out of themselves even by sexuality. What has happened to them? Why are they so completely cut off from life?

When I talk with people about their experience of God, I always ask: Where are you alive? Where can you be touched? If someone then tells me that there is nothing that moves her, I see that I have arrived at a limit. When someone no longer allows himself to be moved, I cannot bring even God to him.

*Inability to be moved by anything, blindness of emotion—that is, no longer being able to feel—this is a rapidly growing phenomenon. Our time is so full of stimuli, impressions, influences—appeals to the senses—but many people find themselves unsure about what they can trust. It is not that we live in a meaningless time—not at all. We are positively bombarded by offers of meaning, but we are completely disoriented: What is reliable? Which is really important? What should I choose? Which path should I follow? What profession should I choose? What am I supposed to do? What relationships should I enter into? The answers all have consequences.*

*Our modern culture seems to promote a particular variant of human history, namely, that of constant progress and upward movement. That path is, however, not very much interested in the common good; it is primarily directed to personal advantage and a contest that marginalizes and exploits other people and the natural bases of our lives. In this race, the danger of loss and separation is great indeed: We lose our link to Nature, our concern for others, and also our sense of the Holy, and we cannot accept anything that is not perfect. We think in either-or categories. We are unable to love anything or anyone we cannot control.*

*How can we escape this narrow way of thinking and open our eyes to the fullness and wholeness of life?*

## Anselm Grün

Overblown images and expectations are certainly a danger: that I always have to be perfect, that I must always have everything in my grasp and under control, that I always have to be "cool." The result is that our souls rebel. Daniel Hell[12] says: depression is often the soul's cry for help in the face of these exaggerated images.

Fear of being boxed in and of having to make a decision also plays its part. There are too many possibilities today, and a decision is always for something and against something. Many people today find this hard. They want to have everything. Then suddenly all the doors are closed, and they have nothing. Jesus says: enter through the narrow gate so that your life will be broad. Out of pure fear of limiting themselves, some people accomplish nothing at all. But life only happens in self-giving, and self-giving is despised nowadays. People prefer to observe, to have everything in hand, to control everything. And yet life only succeeds when I give myself and limit myself. That is: when I limit myself, my life broadens out. Johannes Tauler[13] writes so beautifully: "Every road leads through the bottleneck."

Today I find it is this way: You move along a particular track. Then comes a bottleneck, a canyon, and you jump to another track until another bottleneck occurs, and you leap onto another track. But in that way you never get through the bottleneck or tunnel, and your life never widens out again. You are always living in a preliminary, provisional state. I want to be in control, but because I am so busy controlling, I never get to live.

### David Steindl-Rast

Maybe it is all because of our isolation. That could be one of the roots of our estrangement from others, estrangement even from ourselves and from the divine. Still, I am inclined to say that isolation has something positive about it. It took us centuries to discover, cultivate, and defend our individuality. And that individuality is something positive. On one of my journeys I encountered a culture in which the people had nothing like the individuality we have. There an individual cannot make a decision; it is always the family or the tribe that decides. Then I realized what a treasure we have in our individuality and independence. And yet at the present time, we have driven it too far. I think it will have to get worse before we see how terrible it is for us.

We have neglected the necessary opposite: our network with others. And so we lack relationship. In fact, I reach the highest stage of my self-realization by forging broad and deep relationships. The more relationships I am woven into, the more I become my Self. But we have purchased our independence by cutting off relationships. Now we are on the threshold of a time when we need to lose as little as possible of the valuable independence we have gained but must begin again to link to life-sustaining relationships. That is not only possible but also necessary. We will be all the more independent when we live embedded in relationships. But it seems to me that not enough people understand that.

### Anselm Grün

Carl Gustav Jung said: Jesus individualized people, so follow your own voice. Let the dead bury the dead. Go your own way. In that sense, the idea that each person is unique and independent is altogether Christian.

The other side is certainly our fear of surrender. Psychologists say that we have lost not only our relationship to others but also to ourselves. Absence of relationship is the sickness of our time. I am in relationship neither to my Self nor to things, and then I expect everything from my relationship to the other. Then I cannot forge a relationship to God, either. The important questions, then, are: How can I live relationship? How can I have a sense of relationship?

The third thing is this business of going my own way. Every way is unique; we must not lose that truth. The first monks also took their leave of an extended family that was very narrow. For them, this was a path to liberation, because in that time there was no opportunity for an individual to decide; everything was set in advance. When someone left the extended family and went into the desert to be a monk, he went his own way altogether, while the others continued on the path predetermined for them. But the monks were not satisfied with just leaving; they surrendered themselves to a Greater One, relying totally on God. For Benedict, surrender to God is on the same level as surrender to society and to work.

Today I often find that young people are so anxious about landing in a state of "burnout" that they can't give themselves to their work at all. That is why Benedict tied surrender in prayer to surrender in work: *ora et labora*. It is part of spirituality to free oneself from other people and at the same time to surrender oneself to work.

Ursula Nuber[14] once wrote a book titled *Die Egoismus-Falle* [The egoism trap]. Jesus' central demand is: love your neighbor as yourself. In earlier times people only saw the neighbor; today we are in danger of seeing only ourselves, and suddenly that leads us into isolation.

### David Steindl-Rast

"Love your neighbor as [you love] yourself" is, as I see it, a wrong translation. Correctly rendered from the Hebrew it says explicitly—and I have researched this thoroughly— "Love your neighbor *as* yourself." It would be possible to say in Hebrew "like/as [you love] yourself," but the text avoids that. It says specifically "*as* yourself." There is only *one* Self, and you possess it in common with your neighbor. Love means "saying yes, *living* yes to belonging." The Self is that to which we belong, whether we want to or not. It is a matter of understanding and experiencing that there is only a single Self that expresses itself in so many "I"s—the one Self. All the great spiritual traditions have discovered this. In Hinduism it is called "Atman," in Buddhism, "the Buddha nature" or the "face you had before you were born." In Christianity it is called the "Christ-Self." "Christ lives in me," says Paul. That is *the* Self. The great traditions know it.

"Love your neighbor *as* yourself," then, means: be aware that you and your neighbor are one. Say yes to this belonging-in-Self. Your "I" and the "I" of your neighbor are two different expressions of this one Self. Perhaps we could say that the countless "I"s that exist are all existing because the one great "Self" is so inexhaustible that it wants to express itself ever anew in each individual. That is so important for our personal life as well. We live as "I." My "I" was not yet here ninety years ago, and no one missed it. At one point, it began to exist. And at some point—at a time now easily foreseeable—it will simply no longer be there. But the Self, my Self, is beyond time. The more emphasis I place on the Self, the more I am elevated above the flow of time. The Self is not in time. That is how I see it.

### Anselm Grün

I would not share the idea in Buddhism that the person is completely dissolved. I think that in Christianity the person remains unique, but that, at depth, we are one with the other. This Self, as your Self, means for me that human nature is the same, and therefore we can see ourselves in the other, or—as you say—"Christ" or the "Buddha nature" in us; that I can understand. Still, C. G. Jung says that we have to come from the "I" to the Self. In the Self, God is always also present; the deepest meaning is there.

# Ego, Fear, and Nothingness, or:

## The Epic Discovery of Self

*In the history of Christianity, self-love was long and variously denounced. This attitude missed the truth that a human being must first have or acquire an "I," that is, become self-aware, in order to be able to let go of it and discover the Self. Thus it is important to have an ego and become aware of it; only then is it possible and necessary to leave it behind.*

### Anselm Grün

In the first place, the ego is always present. C. G. Jung says that in the first half of life it is important to develop a strong ego; in the second half one centers on the Self. But that does not mean that the ego is entirely gone. Jesus says: "Deny yourself," which means: distance yourself from your ego. Get free of your ego. But I am skeptical when someone who is on a spiritual path says: I am altogether free of my ego. I am nothing but a self. The danger is that in saying this, one inflates one's ego, feeling oneself to be something special and placing oneself above others.

### David Steindl-Rast

I think we need three concepts: Self, I, and ego. At the moment we are only using two: the Self and the ego. I find it more helpful to say that the Self expresses itself through the I. Sometimes we say "I" and sometimes, when we want to be emphatic, "I myself." That is something totally positive: "I myself." But the "I" can forget the Self. The "I" becomes fearful because it is only a single, isolated "I" among so many others. And out of that fear arises the ego. In the moment in which the "I" forgets the Self, it collapses in on itself, and that is what I call the ego. Ego is characterized by fear, and from fear come aggression, competitiveness, and meanness. Fear that there is not enough, that someone will take something from me creates meanness, miserliness. Competitiveness begins in fear that someone might get ahead of me. Aggression, competitiveness, and meanness are typical of the ego because it has forgotten its Self. At the moment when the "I" remembers the Self again, it need no longer fear because, after all, we are each of us a Self, different expressions of the one Self. When I am not afraid, then violence and rivalry vanish. Now I have respect for others and am prepared to cooperate with them. I can share because we all belong together. The awareness that we are bound together in the Self changes everything in radical fashion.

So, maybe we can agree on a way of speaking that talks of the Self that expresses itself in the "I," in many different, quite unique "I"s, and see the ego only as a falsified form of the "I," a forgetfulness of the Self, a forgetting of who I really am.

### Anselm Grün

All right, I see the ego in two ways. There is the egocentric ego that forgets the Self. But there is also the ego as a drive.

For example, when I preach a sermon, of course I want to be transparent to the spirit of Jesus. But the ego is present because I want to do it well. That is a drive. But I have to make the ego permeable. The ego is not only troubled by anxiety. It is anxious at times when I only revolve around my own ego and feel I have to assert it. But the ego is also a drive that always has to be made permeable. To that extent I have to constantly distance myself from the ego and say: no, it is not about me but about something greater.

### David Steindl-Rast

I agree entirely, but I would express it somewhat differently. We need an expression for the negative, and I call that "ego." The other is what I would call my proper "I-awareness," a consciousness of my uniqueness, my interests, my gifts, and my difficulties as well. If Helen Keller[15] had not been blind, she would never have become such a great teacher. I do agree with you: we need this drive. That must be said. The "I" that is transparent to the drive is, in fact, self-aware in the fullest sense of the word.

*The difference I have perceived between the two of you has to do with the concept of the Self. From you, Brother David, I hear that fundamentally we are all one Self, while from Father Anselm I hear that there is a distinction between the ego and the Self—the Self is still my Self, but in awareness of my Self I can achieve a union with the Self of the other. So there is connection in the Self, but in the ego there is a separation. Have I understood that correctly?*

### Anselm Grün

Yes, I would call the Self the center where I am one and am joined with others. But I would again describe us as this unique image of God, that every human being is a unique image, that every human being expresses God in a unique way—that is similar to your viewpoint. Each is a unique image of God, but each expresses God. And you say too: each of us expresses the Self, and the Self is ultimately our divine image.

### David Steindl-Rast

Yes, the Self is the divine Self. But I want to ask about something you mentioned briefly: when I find myself, I also find God. What did you mean by that?

### Anselm Grün

When I ask: "Who am I really?" I am not getting only at my life history, my childhood, and everything else, but also asking, "Who am I?" That "I" is ultimately a mystery that I cannot describe any more than I can describe God. The Old Testament prohibition against making an image of God applies ultimately to the "I" as well. I say that God has made an image of me for Godself, but that image is something I cannot describe. In Luke 24, after the resurrection, Jesus says: *"Egō eimi autos*—"I am myself" (Luke 24:39). The exegetes pass over this, but *autos* ("self") was, for Stoic philosophy, the innermost sanctuary of the human. I sometimes give people an exercise: to say to themselves again and again, throughout the day, at every opportunity, "I am myself." That way I quickly become aware of how often I am not myself but am playing a role and trying to prove myself. I am myself: if I meditate on that over and over again, I stumble upon the divine, but I cannot describe it. I only have a sense of it.

### David Steindl-Rast

We are a mystery to ourselves. I will go one step further, with Martin Buber[16] and Ferdinand Ebner,[17] and say that through you I am I. That is what the American poet e. e. cummings said: "I am through you so I." At the moment when I say "I," I presuppose a "you"—not a conglomerate of the many "you"s I meet in my life; my great "you" is not a generalization of the many but precedes them all and goes beyond them all. We can also recognize this in the fact that none of our encounters really and ultimately satisfies us. Perhaps for a moment, but then, sooner or later, that "you" dies. We are oriented to a "You" beyond time. That is the divine "You." We never find it completely realized in this life.

*What shows us that we are oriented to a "You" beyond time? Imagine an agnostic who would say, "What are you talking about? I don't feel it." For an agnostic that is a pure assertion.*

### David Steindl-Rast

Simply to say "I" presupposes a "you." Every human being, as an "I," is oriented to a "you." So you might ask: have you ever completely encountered that "you" in reality?

### Anselm Grün

I would get to the same result from a different starting point. Every human being longs to love and be loved. On that journey we have experiences of fulfillment and disappointment, enchantment and wounding. It will never be that anyone loves me in such a way that I am satisfied. The goal is not just to love and be loved through fulfillment and disappointment but to *be* love and *become* love. Then, in the depth of my soul, I discover the source of love, which ultimately is God.

Of course, one may object: "That is only wishful thinking. We want that, but in reality that pure love does not exist." I would answer with an experience a woman once told me about: "I was meditating, and suddenly I was love. It was not love for a particular person, but love simply streamed out of me, into my room, to the flowers, to the animals, to people, out into Nature." Sometimes we have such experiences of unity. But those who have not yet experienced such unity have a hard time understanding it.

### David Steindl-Rast

That I find satisfying. That, taken from experience, is convincing. I believe it is also the answer I would give the agnostic: if you cannot see it yet, you don't have to accept it. Wait until you experience it. It is not a dogmatic principle we want to impose on you. We only want to say that millions of people experience it. You can too. Open yourself to it.

I have found one other way to introduce people to this directedness to the divine "You": we can become aware that we do not experience our lives as a succession of events but as a life story. That is because we are constantly telling our story to a "You." But we never find this "You" to whom we tell our story as a reality in space and time. Even when we try to tell our deepest experience to our dearest friends, it never quite succeeds. It seems to be made for our eternal "You."

That reminds me of something that happened with Henri Nouwen,[18] whom I knew well. He traveled a lot and had a great circle of students who loved and revered him. Those were the days when people made slides of their trips and showed them. After thirty slides, the students began to be a little bored. So sometimes he would say: "I know what it will be like when I get to heaven. God will say: 'Henri, here you are! Show me your slides!'" We all wish for that. We long for the great "You" who wants to hear our life story and who also understands it.

# What Self Do We Want to Radiate? or:

## Calling, Courage, and Fear

*Who am I, really? What should I do? What am I good for in this world?—People, especially at midlife, find that their "tower of life" is built. Life goes its own way. Is there something else? It is then that the question of one's real calling may arise. What calls me? How do I manage to hear the call and respond to it? How do I open myself to the call, so that I can follow it?*

### Anselm Grün

Each one's life traces its mark on this world. You don't have to do anything great. You get up every morning, you talk with people. You have a "vibe." What do you want to transmit? Bitterness, dissatisfaction, loneliness, or understanding, warmth, and love? None of that requires any great achievement. It simply happens in the way I live my life. From quantum physics we know that all things are linked together. The mark I trace helps to shape the world. The second question is: What is my duty? What is my mission? Do I sense something there? Again, the mission need not be anything unusual: being a father or mother, my job, linking and networking people together in the circles where I find myself. Some may have a special calling: to go to Africa or somewhere else. But it need not always be such a great thing. In German, we do not speak of one's "job" but of one's "calling" (*Beruf*), which has to do with being called. A calling can also be a call. Those are the two ways: living my life and carving a trace there and trusting that it will make the world a little brighter, and a calling that has to do with being called. A woman who suffered from depression once asked me: "What kind of mark can I carve in the world? I can't even get right with myself." I told her: "No one expects a trace of joyfulness from you, but if you say 'yes' to your depression, you will give off a sense of the mystery that life is something deeper and also has its dark side, together with a smidgen of hope." That is important: what kind of mark do I want to carve? The second is then the calling, the sending from without.

### David Steindl-Rast

That makes complete sense to me. In my own experience I have discovered three questions I have to ask myself when I don't know what I ought to do, whether it be a small decision or a really big one.

The first thing I ask myself is: What would make me happy? That brings out what is unique and best in me. What would make me really happy?

The second question (within the framework of what would make me truly happy): What are my gifts? It is amazing that people often want to do something for which they really have no gift. People want to do something but have no talent for it at all. I, for example, would really love to be able to whiz around on inline skates. It seems as if it would be heaven to swoop around like that. Sometimes I dream about it. But I have no talent for it. So: What would make me really happy, and what *can* I do?

Then comes the third and most important question: What does life offer me? And here my calling comes into play. Life calls out to me, offers me this opportunity that I have to seize by the forelock. My cooperation with what this mysterious, always surprising life offers me from moment to moment—it all depends on that.

*But in order to ask these questions, some have to get out of their fearful mode. Many people remain stuck in a groove of doing and doing more and more, which doesn't work any longer because there is fear underlying it: if something else appears behind it, something that really calls to me, then I have to let go of something. And then maybe something I have built in my life will collapse. But I can't deal with that. It may be material security or a relationship, or whatever: the greatest enemy of freedom and its call is the fear that cuts us down. What are your experiences of that?*

### Anselm Grün

On the one hand, there is fear of limitation and of having to let go of certain things we are used to. Many people have established themselves in their lives. They would like to do something, maybe go to Africa—but then I couldn't go on vacation or visit with my friends! So we have established ourselves so firmly in our habits that, while we would like to do something, we don't want to let go. For a decision in favor of something is also a decision to let go of something, be it habits or relationships. So now I am afraid. I have settled myself comfortably in life and think that is all that is necessary. Then I dream of great things, but—when you ask,

"What makes me happy?"—then I think of the little joys I don't want to let go of for the sake of the greater happiness.

### David Steindl-Rast

I find it helpful to distinguish between anxiety and fear. Anxiety, as its name says, comes from narrowness, confinement. Anxiety is unavoidable in life, and it is somehow linked to the memory of the narrow birth canal. That is especially significant for me because my mother had a dreadful time giving birth to me; they say it took nearly two days. This unconscious anxiety is still latent in me. And then, finally, I came out right hand first—disgusting.

Again and again in life we get into constricted situations; it can't be avoided. But being afraid means struggling against that constriction. Resistance to anxiety is fear: I don't want to be anxious. Courage is also associated with anxiety. No one can be courageous unless she or he is anxious. But courage accepts anxiety. One who is courageous has anxiety but does not succumb to it. Yes, I am in a confined situation, and I have to get through it into a broader place. That is courage.

That is why I think it is important to distinguish anxiety from fear. But how can we overcome fear, even though we remain anxious? My answer is: all fear is one. When here or there someone overcomes a little bit of fear one has already begun to conquer all fear. Confront your anxiety where you dare to do it.

We learned that as children: when our parents sent us into the dark cellar or the dim garden shed to get something, we gradually came to realize that none of the things we were afraid of really happened. So it is a matter of over-coming fear step-by-step by learning to accept as much anxiety as we are able to at any given time. Then we can say: yes, I admit it, I am anxious, but courage will take it away. It helps to know that fear is a resistance to anxiety. So "fear not!" means "take courage, and take anxiety as it comes!"

### Anselm Grün

When I talk with people I often come across an anxiety about embarrassing oneself, making mistakes, the anxiety that one will be rejected or fail. People have very distinct pictures of all that. In that case anxiety would be an invitation to change my attitude. I don't have to be loved by everybody. I don't have to be perfect. Anxiety is an invitation to be a human being with my own limitations.

### David Steindl-Rast

I have to admit that the image of confinement doesn't fit so well in that context. Maybe we could get around it by saying: whenever we are confronted by anxiety we feel pressure on our rib cage. We have a physical sense of anxiety. But not to give in to it is fearlessness. When I resist, I say, "I can't." And that makes me feel small in all those cases you mention. I feel as if I've been driven into a corner, as we say, and I withdraw instead of finding the way to openness and freedom precisely through the narrow way. "Constriction *is* the way," Kierkegaard says.

*Nowadays there is pressure stemming from all the great opportunities for freedom. We see it, for example, in the "business of self-fulfillment," which postulates: "You have to fulfill yourself! Your life is a project, and you have to make something of yourself." The background of that imperative is the idea that life is the only opportunity. Marianne Gronemeyer has written a book about it.[19] This imperative contains a hidden threat: if you don't take this in hand right now, if you make nothing of yourself, you have lost and you are expendable.[20] This extreme* carpe diem *(seize the day) can push many people into deep despair. The call to self-perfection[21] is enormously exhausting, and that pressure may be one of the reasons why many people experience spiritual burnout. Do you see anything that can take away the pressure to make something of oneself and perfect oneself?*

### Anselm Grün

The demand to always be perfect creates anxiety. It makes me live in constant fear: I can't do it. My project is not good enough. So I create a better and better public image; I have to present myself that way. Anxiety reveals the excessive demands I make on life. My project need not be the best. But many cling to the idea that their project has to be the best. They want to push down their anxiety, either by psychopharmacological means or spiritual suppression. But it doesn't work. I can only transform anxiety if I transform my own attitude: I need not have the best project on earth.

When people are anxious about their own average condition, I say: You must feel sad that you are the way you are and not the best in the world. So you have to get through the pain and then say "yes" to yourself. Inflated images create anxiety. A lot of people want to cling to the images and at the same time get rid of their anxiety. But alas, that doesn't work. I can only overcome anxiety if I say goodbye to the images. Anxiety is an invitation to me to take my leave of inflated images.

## David Steindl-Rast

I am especially fond of the idea of transforming anxiety. Courage transforms anxiety. It does not struggle against it but transforms it. It transforms the stone over which we would otherwise stumble into a stone upon which we can climb a step higher. In connection with the question of meaning that idea says to me that this is about the opportunity that is now offered me. How do I deal with it? We want to find meaning, but usually we forget the necessary distinction between goal and meaning. When I want to attain something and have to work for it, that involves a goal. But play has meaning and need not achieve anything else. We don't dance in order to attain a goal. We play music just to play music. There is no goal at the end. The distinction between meaning and goal, I think, offers us a convenient angle from which to look at the attitude you have described. We play with life. If it is meaningful, it needs no goal. Or it can be goal driven. We have many goals in life that we need to endow with meaning by linking our attitude to work with our attitude to play. When work proceeds in a playful way, it has meaning. As long as it remains nothing but work it is drudgery.

*I want to address a dimension we mentioned earlier, that is, the relationship between ego and Self. What is it that makes us anxious when we are trapped in anxiety? Why is that?*

## David Steindl-Rast

The "I" also has its anxiety, but the ego is characterized by the fact that it fears. When I am afraid, I know that it is not my "I"-Self that is speaking but my ego. The ego fears because it feels itself alone. The ego has forgotten its relationship to the Self, and so it begins to shrink together, away from the "I" into the ego. Because it thinks it is alone, it suffers anxiety. There are all those others who could threaten me. I have to arm myself for the "life struggle." There is not enough available for so many people. How can I get ahead? I have to step over the others and grab for myself whatever I can get. These attitudes are all too evident in our society.

## Anselm Grün

Or the ego constantly tries to impose itself and feels anxiety that it cannot impose itself enough. The ego is always struggling for recognition and affirmation, validity and concern. All those are external things.

*The philosopher Martin Heidegger distinguishes between the "authentic" and the "inauthentic" Self.[22] This is about one's own life: that is, getting away from the "one"—what one thinks, what one does, etc. It is about independence or self-dependence in the literal sense: being able to stand by oneself. That means at the same time that I need something on which I can stand, something that sustains me. I can't stand on the "one." That changes with time and collective moods and modes. So I need something deeper because otherwise I have no independence.*

## David Steindl-Rast

That is well said: "the authentic and the inauthentic life." I have never used those terms, but I would like to adopt them. The genuine "I" is the "I"-Self, and the inauthentic, what I myself really am not, is the ego.

## Anselm Grün

So I distinguish between change and transformation. Nowadays projects for change are constantly emerging on the scene in esoterics and psychology. I know people who have been changing themselves constantly for ten years and yet remain the same because there is something aggressive in changing oneself: I have to be different, be another person. In changing, I measure myself by external standards: I have to be like this one or as successful as that one. Change is always aimed at imitation. Transformation, though, means that I value myself as what I have become. Everything is possible, but the genuine has not yet emerged. By the genuine I mean being entirely myself or, in religious terms, becoming the unique image of God. The goal of transformation is for the genuine to emerge.

There is a wonderful rabbinic story that illustrates this important difference. A rabbi prays: "O God, make me like Abraham." The voice of God says: "I already have an Abraham. I want you!"

# Goodbye to Infantile Images of God, or:

## In Search of the Divine Mystery

*From the beginnings of culture, people have tried to enter into dialogue with the powers they sense as divine. They have experienced Nature as numinous and have interpreted thunder, lightning, earthquakes, rain, and floods, etc., as the products of a divine force working everywhere. Later, they even gave names to these natural phenomena and sacrificed animals, plants, and human beings to these gods. They feared and worshiped the gods. But those forms of sacrificial religion also divided people and drove them to war: Which god is the stronger? Mine or yours? Violence was exercised in the name of one's own god, and power structures were established. What images of God are responsible for this, and what images of God would instead strengthen life-affirming forces?*

### Anselm Grün

In the beginning, the Jews had their own war god who was stronger than all the others. But later, and still within Israel, that God was spiritualized. God is the God of all people. There is not a tribal god I can use for myself and my people. God is the father of us all. We don't need to appease God. We need have no fear that God will injure us. God as *tremendum* means being touched by him, having reverence. Ultimately anxiety in the face of God, the demonic god, is anxiety about myself, the demons in my soul. Those are often projected onto God. For me, God is the God of all people, whom I cannot possess and who liberates me. Everything can exist before his face. I need project nothing negative onto him. My experience in spiritual direction tells me that our Self-image and our God-image correspond. If someone has an image of a punishing God, there is little sense in holding a theoretical discussion with her. Instead, I ask: Why do you feel you have to punish yourself? Are you so fearful of your own psyche, the tendencies in your soul? Do you have to be so controlling because you are afraid? That is what it is all about. God is the one before whom I can expose my whole truth. I need have no fear of anything in myself; I am unconditionally loved.

### David Steindl-Rast

It seems to me that the answer to the question of why people punish themselves has to do with the fact that they have internalized an anxiety someone has imposed on them. You have identified with someone who made you anxious. So I come back to the original question. I think that the picture of early religion, while quite commonly accepted, is a misunderstanding. The so-called primitives who, for example, worship the sun are much more aware that the sun is only an image of the divine than the anthropologists who accuse them of worshiping the sun as a god. I think there are no idol worshipers; those are always the "others." If we pray before St. Anthony, it is just the same as when a Hindu prays before Ganesha. People may prefer to pray before a certain statue, but that does not mean they *pray to* the statue. We find this demonization of idols already in the psalms. Trying to make an image for ourselves is something more internal. We can see the external: there is something made of wood, gold, or stone. But the image of God we have within us can very easily become an idol, and that is what it is as long as we cling to it without changing.

### Anselm Grün

When the Bible speaks of a punishing God, that certainly means something, but not that God is one who punishes arbitrarily. Instead, it simply means that life is the way it is. The world is the way it is. You can't simply live as you want to, against nature. Punishment is the consequence of reality.

*Could we say that when speaking of God as judge we should not misunderstand it in a juridical sense but say that God judges by bringing order to something?*

### David Steindl-Rast

We also say: "Daddy will be the judge of that," and we mean "put it in order" or "restore" it. When God appears as judge, God puts the world right.

### Anselm Grün

It can also mean "straighten out" or "direct." Judgment is meant to direct us toward God. Albert Görres[23] says we must guard against infantile images. They are images of our own reality, but we dare not project them onto God as a petty judge.

## David Steindl-Rast

You said it before: life is the great mystery. And life has a direction: one can be affirming or rejecting of life. What that means in individual cases can only be decided in those individual cases, but we know that life has a direction and is intended for something. Therefore we can also speak of the will of God. Life, though this is only an image, is still the best, the closest match for the Mystery we call God. The biblical tradition speaks again and again of the "living God, the "God of life.""

*If we speak of God's judging in the sense of "bringing order into things," then what would be God's justice, on which generations of oppressed people have always relied? They believe that God will overcome the evil under which they have suffered. Countless people have been killed and tortured, have been allowed to starve; they have been excluded and forgotten and tossed onto the "dungheap of history" by the mighty. This cry of the outraged must not fall silent. They want to have justice, as much as that can be achieved in this life, but if not, at least in eternal life.*

## Anselm Grün

The psalms beg God to bring justice now. That is important. The Jewish philosopher Max Horkheimer[24] says that there is a basic law in the human soul that murderers must not triumph over their victims. The image of the last judgment affirms that; it means to say that no perpetrator can go to God unjudged. But judgment is also the hope that each one can be put in order. If an individual allows himself to be put right, then the perpetrator and the victim can live together again—if they let themselves be put right before God. But both must be put right and judged if a common life is to be possible. Many people criticize that as putting everything off to some future time. Therefore it is important to see that the psalms cry for justice here. And that is why the church has to be an active advocate for justice in this world. It must not simply pray but also struggle. The last judgment itself is only an image of hope . . .

### David Steindl-Rast

. . . for the poor! An image of hope for the poor and a horror to the rich when they use their financial power to oppress, exploit, and create injustice—but not because they have a lot of money. There are many rich people who are poor and many poor who are rich. Krister Stendahl,[25] a Lutheran bishop from Sweden and a marvelous exegete, always says, "When the pericopes about judgment are read, the poor who long for justice rejoice, and the oppressors shudder." And that is how it should be.

*What would make the oppressors shudder? Today someone who is totally secularized would say that the last judgment is an unprovable myth and is irrelevant. What should she be afraid of?*

## David Steindl-Rast

Life—and not some God who sits in heaven and then comes down and punishes—only permits things that are life-affirming. Whoever does something that rejects life always has a bad conscience somehow, because we human beings have a sense that life demands justice. Martin Luther King Jr. said it this way: "The arc of the moral universe is long, but it bends toward justice."

*I want to put this question in even sharper terms. For example, when I think of the military dictatorships that dominated nearly every country in Latin America from 1965 to 1985—how many generals and torturers escaped unscathed! First they were protected by the court system, then perhaps they were sentenced when they were very old, but they showed no regret in public over their behavior, or else they died soon after. When we know how many thousands of people were "disappeared" in those years, were tortured, killed, it is a slap in the face of the victims to see that their torturers never even had a bad conscience about it or maybe justified what they had done because supposedly they had protected their countries from Communism.*

## Anselm Grün

When someone kills another, he always kills something in himself. No one can be unjust and remain immune. Somehow the deed will avenge itself. Outwardly the perpetrators may seem to have come through unscathed and felt themselves to be the victors, even into their old age. But their souls were demolished, nonetheless. And then this last judgment is often the last hope for the victims that no one will get to God unscathed by escaping the truth. We find this tension in the psalms: Why do things go so badly for good people and so well for the evil ones? That is a fundamental question the psalmists struggle with. But they say: you will be justified. It is all about suffering this injustice and hoping that God will create justice even now—but at the latest in the eternal judgment.

### David Steindl-Rast

The answer you suggest for the question of injustice ultimately means that we do not see enough. I agree with you. There is something in me that I hope to overcome, that cries out: they should be punished. And there is something in me that is sustained by more love: for it is both the greatest punishment and the greatest gift to be shown how wrong our deed was and to repent. Of course we cannot prove that, but we hope and trust because that leads us more in the direction of life. We do not know what happens in death. An instant can contain a whole life. At the moment of death, it may be that your whole life breaks apart and that you see what you have done wrong and regret it at depth. I believe that this regret lies deep in the human if she only sees clearly enough. When she sees it, that is the greatest punishment and at the same time her repentance. That could be how God judges.

*Let me provoke you one more time: the Chilean General Pinochet attended a Catholic church, both when he was dictator and later as a convicted criminal; he received Communion and presumably did not feel guilty about it.*

## Anselm Grün

He did that outwardly, and he considered himself a good Catholic. But surely something was dead in his soul. No one can live against the truth for a long time and remain untouched. At some time or other the inner fragmentation will emerge, even if I present myself outwardly as correct, at the latest in death. No one can get to God by evading his own truth. No one can avoid pain for what has gone wrong. Karl Rahner[26] says: in death the soul can have complete control of itself, and then it recognizes all truth. Here we can only see part of the truth. The more we have lived in avoidance of ourselves, the more painful it will be. At the same time there is hope that even the unjust can still repent, but they will not do so by evading pain and truth.

## David Steindl-Rast

We really have to insist that the examples we are talking about are scandalous. This injustice is unspeakable . . .

*And I haven't even mentioned Hitler, who marked our history in Germany and Austria so deeply, or Stalin and his murderous deeds.*

## David Steindl-Rast

Indeed. But let's get back again to the Self, the "I," and the ego. I find this image fits: the single Self is like a puppeteer who plays with a lot of puppets. Those are our roles. Our role begins when we are conceived and ends when we die. Then the Self lays aside its puppets. Then my "I" no longer plays a role, and my Self sees what I have done. And then I can laugh or weep, be judged and set right. That's how I picture it to myself.

# Capital Confusions, or:

*On the Temptation to Want to Possess the Truth*

*Talking about God nowadays is problematic in at least two ways: when we think we know exactly who God is, what God wants of human beings, and how life and society, therefore, ought to be shaped—that is the fundamentalist temptation. Those who think they alone possess the truth about God are inclined to impose their ideas at any price, even that of violence, and to force it on others. The second problematic way of talking about God is the opposite: to be entirely silent about God, to avoid thinking about God, to deny God or not even to pose the question. Is there a third way between the temptation to possess the truth and the temptation to total negation and suppression of God?*

## David Steindl-Rast

I would say it very simply: the third way is to be genuinely alive. The fundamentalists are not alive, because life is fleeting and always surprising. They close themselves totally to that. The others, who simply do not think about this question, are not alive because they close themselves to the deepest reality of life and do not face life's mystery. If we are really alive, we are awake to the mystery, but at the same time we acknowledge the surprising character of life—of the living God.

But it is not even necessary to speak explicitly about God. Many people who constantly have God on their lips are not talking about God but about their own idols. Other people who don't want to know anything about God, who never use the word "God," can be genuine believers. Faith is not holding something to be true or having God on one's lips. Faith means trust—ultimately in life. When we trust life, we trust the source of life. That is God, the divine source of being alive.

### Anselm Grün

When someone says she doesn't believe in God, I ask: which god don't you believe in . . . ?

We have to reject certain images of God. You speak of life: I would rather speak with Karl Rahner about mystery. Mystery describes something that is greater than myself and that I cannot grasp. Then we are getting to beauty. When I listen to music, I encounter the Mystery. When I go into Nature, I can experience it. Being able to be astonished, being moved and seized by the Mystery—those would be signs for me that someone believes. The fundamentalists separate other people into believers and nonbelievers. But every one of us is believing and nonbelieving. Each of us has a godless side, and doubt is also part of faith. Doubt purifies faith, so that I don't identify God with my images of God but always question: Who is this God? We need images of God; otherwise we could not speak about God. But at the same time we have to know that God is beyond all images.

### David Steindl-Rast

Just as anxiety is part of courage, so doubt is part of faith. Suzuki Roshi[27] once gave a long lecture on faith. As a young student I would not have thought it possible for a Buddhist teacher to talk about faith. He quite rightly spoke about trust and said that the opposite of faith is fear. He said: "Don't be upset if you are afraid. That is like the wind in your face when you ride your bike very fast. Pat yourself on the back and be proud that you have so much anxiety, because it is faith that creates that anxiety. But if you have courage, you can overcome it. As long as your courage is only a nose ahead of the anxiety you are a believer."

*Let me take up what you said about images of God one more time, because that is a very important point. When we talk about atheism today, it may be that what is going on is really shadow boxing between different images of God that are unworthy of belief and that an honest, believing atheist rejects. Because of his rationality he thinks it unworthy to believe in a particular image of God. We can learn a great deal from well-informed atheists. I think it is a great wisdom teaching of the Bible that it forbids the making of images, a prohibition we also find in Islam. It is aware of the danger of deceit and illusion that accompanies human images of God. How can we experience God beyond these images today?*

### Anselm Grün

It is always important to discuss with an atheist what she does not believe. Usually she has an image of God that is too trivial and narrow. She thinks of God as something that is[28] and not as Being, to use Heidegger's terms. The paradox is that God is a mystery that is beyond us, and in spite of that, we Christians have the courage to address that Mystery as "thou." But God is not a concrete person we can pin down; rather, this incredible Mystery can touch me like a "thou" who addresses me, as Martin Buber says: Then God is not only the depth of being. I always reject the idea that "God is nothing but the ground of being." God is the ground of being. But God is also love, the energy in us and in all things, and at the same time, God is always even more. No statement about God can pin down the Mystery; it has to remain open. Max Horkheimer says that churches have the duty to keep alive the yearning for the Wholly Other, and in doing so, they make an important contribution to the humanization of society. For society has totalitarian features. It would like to take complete control over people. God is the one who lets us breathe freely, with whom a person is not tied to a purpose. Nowadays everything is determined from an economic perspective. We are experiencing a totalization of the economy, yet God is the free space that lets us breathe.

*So-called "negative theology"[29] attempts to say something about God by saying what God is not. God is not this way, or that way. . . . But how can we say that God is not this or that? I need an experience on which to found my (not) knowing.*

### Anselm Grün

That is an experience one can only sense from afar. It is indescribable, and yet this Indescribable, Ungraspable is an experience that touches me at depth. Contemplative monks speak of it this way: I look into and through it, but I don't see anything in particular. That is a moment like a Buddhist enlightenment, when one arrives at an inner clarity.

**David Steindl-Rast**

That is the real answer to the question why the advocates of different God-images are at odds: because they do not speak out of experience and intuition but out of conceptuality. They think they grasp it. But what we can grasp is certainly not God, since by definition God is the Mystery. Mystics of all traditions agree absolutely on that point because they speak out of experience and intuition. To have that experience, you need to take time. So: meditation. But even very busy people receive this gift again and again. A mother who cares for her children all day long has no time for meditation. She looks at her child with love, and the child looks at its mother: that is already an encounter and experience out of which bursts this deeper ground beyond all naming. That is a touch of the Unutterable.

Normally I would say that people should build daily meditation into their lives in order to be truly human. How they do it depends on their individual personalities and the circumstances of their lives. But a great many people who could never speak of it because they lack the education and vocabulary know all this much better than we who can talk so cleverly about it. The farmers' children and shepherds who herd their flocks under the open sky and sit at night by firelight experience profound encounters with an incomprehensible reality. It is a part of being human, at every level; it is not just something for the educated who can take time for it and have enough money to afford to make a spiritual retreat.

May I add something to what we touched on before?—namely, that God is often used by those in authority to strike fear into us. Authoritarian powers are always busy making people afraid, because then they are compliant. Why is the divine Mystery so well suited for exciting fear? Because a shudder is part of the experience of the Holy. The Holy fascinates us and makes us shiver, so that we are right to speak of fearing God. But that shuddering is misused to make people afraid, and it has been misused this way with enormous frequency in the course of history. But reverence before God and courage in the face of human beings are inseparable. Rightly understood, fear of God is the obverse of the courage to engage fully on behalf of justice.

# "Dead Man Rising," or:

## *Jesus Christ and the Buddha*

*Christians believe that Jesus is more than just one among many religious founders. They believe that Jesus is the Son of God, that God's Self became human in this historical Jesus, the carpenter from Nazareth, for the salvation of all. They even believe that this same one who was crucified was raised by God from the dead and will return at the end of days to judge the living and the dead. This Christian faith has to make a Muslim or a Jew, who also believe in God, to say nothing of a humanistic agnostic or an atheist, shake her head. It must seem completely absurd to them. Is it even possible to communicate this core of Christian faith by rational means? Or must we say to our contemporaries who think themselves enlightened: "Such faith convictions belong in the realm of myth. Jesus may have been the historical model of an outstanding human being, of which there have been several in the course of history. But everything beyond that is pious legend"?*

### Anselm Grün

There is a tendency nowadays to nail Jesus down: Jesus was nothing but a human being with a particular religious gift or a religious founder. That is a way to free ourselves from his demands, to objectify him and judge him by contemporary and temporal standards and what I find acceptable or not. For me, dogmatic theology is the art of keeping

51

the mystery open. When I say "Jesus was the Son of God," I am far from knowing what that means, but I keep the mystery open—and the demand as well. I cannot get away from Jesus' demand. The words of Jesus have an absolute claim on me. Of course, I have to try to understand them over and over again in the given context. That Jesus is the Son of God is a mystery. Heinrich Böll,[30] who was certainly no conservative but a skeptical Christian, said: For me, it is important that Jesus was not only a human being but also the Son of God; otherwise it is all a romantic tale.

Jesus was fully and entirely a human being, and when we speak of him as "Son of God," we are talking about the demand God speaks to us through him. We can't bend those words to suit ourselves: they confront us. That is the demand: God speaks to us through the human being. Karl Rahner called Jesus "God's absolute self-communication." God has communicated God's self in different ways but does so absolutely in Jesus. This is a mystery we can never fully explain, but it is important to me to let the mystery stand.

God withdraws from us again and again. Even in meditation I have to ask myself over and over whether that is an idea or a projection. Jesus confronts us concretely. When I read or hear his words, God becomes more concrete to me. Of course, I cannot see God directly. Jesus said: "Whoever sees me, sees the Father" (John 12:45), but that, too, is a mystery. And yet God is more concrete through Jesus and is no longer a plaything of my own projections, in which I imagine God according to my own ideas. He encounters me, calls me out of myself, makes me insecure. Jesus is for me a figure who is entirely present and whom I cannot bypass.

**David Steindl-Rast**

I would see it as important to ask first of all what the Christian tradition means when it says "Jesus is the Son of God." I find it problematic just to fling the dogma at someone's head. First we have to ask what "Son of God" means, and that is primarily an exegetical question that I won't go into. After that I would suggest two steps: first, because we are being asked as Christians, I would answer from Christian tradition, and in that context we find an important place in Jesus' genealogy in Luke (Luke 3:23-38).

Luke traces Jesus' descent through multiple ancestors back to "Adam, the son of God" (Luke 3:38). Adam is not the name of the first human being; "Adam" simply means "human being." *We* are Adam. So *we* are "the son of God." That is the starting point. If we are called "son of God," the next question is: how can we know what it means to be "son of God"? And the answer: we know it from our experience. We are the children of life. Life brings us forth, and like a mother it always gives us exactly what we need. But life is an encounter with the unfathomable Mystery we call God.

So if we are all children of God, why shouldn't Jesus be Son of God? Then comes the question: is he not Son of God in a unique way? To which I would say: certainly in a unique way, first because each of us is uniquely "son of God." We are all unique. Second, Jesus is yet "more" unique because he is the impulse for us to reflect on what it means to be son of God. That, too, is a great uniqueness.

Then we also have to distinguish between Jesus and Christ. It is no accident that the New Testament sometimes says "Jesus" and sometimes "Christ." I understand that to mean that Jesus is in every way a human being like us—as Christian dogma says—but Christ is the Self common to us all. Jesus is the "I" of Jesus; Christ is the Self—our Self and the Self of Jesus. We must not casually dump that distinction. Some things can only be said about Christ, others only about Jesus; otherwise confusion arises. It can be very helpful to consider the distinction. Some people find it easier to approach Jesus, others Christ. Christ is a reality I can find in myself, my Self.

Jesus, on the other hand, is one human being among other human beings in world history. We, as Christians, hold the two together. We believe in Jesus Christ. If it was only about the Christ in us, we would have nothing against which to test our ideas about the Christ-reality. If it was only about Jesus, a single person, he could at best be an external model for me. But when I hold the two together I see and recognize in Jesus Christ the measure of my own complete becoming-myself. We as Christians can understand his uniqueness from this point of view as well. I am bound to Christ in my innermost being.

### Anselm Grün

"Son of God" can be explained in different ways. After all, the Jews call David and the kings "sons of God." Being a son of God means being God's beloved. The Greeks, though— they expressed it in terms of "being." Jesus "is" Son of God. There were exegetes who said that falsified the meaning. I don't think so—but still, it is a mystery. Of course, Jesus was a historical figure and wholly and entirely a human being, as the dogma about him says. In him, God and the human are unmixed and unseparated. That is a great wisdom. He is totally and entirely a human being, and still God is wholly and entirely in him. We have to maintain that tension. I have read quite a few Jesus books. For one author he is a rebel, for another a religious founder, for still others a religiously gifted person. But all those are attempts to categorize him and also, ultimately, to escape his claim. So he is judged like any other historical figure, and I can say what I like about him and what I don't like. When we say he is Son of God, then no one can say, "I like this; I don't like that," because that statement is wholly and entirely a claim on me.

### David Steindl-Rast

I agree completely, but it is a question of *how* we say it. That is what we are struggling with now. There is a level of discussion on which we can say that he is a historical person like others because he is a human being like others. When we admit that, we gain goodwill and lose nothing by it. But now we say: there is much more at stake. Then we enter on a different level of the discussion. Now we want to say something about Jesus the human being and at the same time about ourselves: we are *all* son of God. That is important. The historical Jesus helped us all to see what "son of God" means. That opens up opportunities for us to engage in dialogue with other traditions because we don't want to force anything on them with our dogma. Instead, we say: from your own religious experience you can comprehend what "son of God" could mean for you. Every tradition attempts to express in its own way the relationship between us human beings and ultimate reality; we Christians express it this way: Jesus Christ is (and we all are) "son of God."

*That of course arouses resistance in me. If I were to represent the fundamentalists, I would argue: "You know what the Bible says: 'No one comes to the Father except through me' (John 14:6)."*

### Anselm Grün

Karl Rahner interpreted that passage very well.[31] C. G. Jung said: Jesus was a human being, but he activated the Self in the human. He became the archetype of the Self. And Rahner says: everyone who follows his conscience—no matter what his religion—will encounter God in death and also the image of Jesus he has unknowingly seen. Rahner sought to prove from philosophy that the human being includes the thought of God as horizon in every act of thinking. And it belongs to humans' innermost knowledge that God acts in history, and that it is therefore probable that God acts historically in one human being—that God takes on human form. In death, each of us will understand that. In death we will know God and recognize the mystery of Jesus that we have been seeking without knowing it.

If we surrender ourselves to this Jesus, who fulfills our deepest longing for the image of God, then Jesus is the way to the Father.

*Jesus says: "I am the way, and the truth, and the life." Doesn't he mean that in an exclusive sense?*

### Anselm Grün

No. None of the words of the Bible may be read in an exclusive sense; they are positive affirmations. We can understand this saying to mean: when I look at Jesus, concern myself with him, I begin to see the truth. Truth in Greek is *alētheia*, which means "unhiddenness." That means that the veil over things will be drawn aside, and I will see beyond it. Then I find a way; then I find life. I can also interpret it in the opposite way: wherever I see the truth, where I am alive, I have a sense of Jesus; I encounter Jesus. When God says in the Old Testament: "I have called you by name, you are mine. . . . I give people in return for you" (Isa 43:1-4), that is a positive affirmation and not one that excludes other nations in principle. It says nothing negative about others.

### David Steindl-Rast

When I listen to you sympathetically, I can accept it when you say, "I encounter Jesus." But the saying "I am the way, and the truth, and the life" comes from John's gospel (John 14:6), which speaks of Jesus Christ with a strong emphasis on *Christ*. At that point I would have said, "I encounter Christ."

The way we are talking about here is the way to God, the way into the Great Mystery. Whoever is on that way is realizing the Christ-Self. When Jesus Christ says in John, "I am the way," that does not mean: "I am the only way among all others that leads to the goal." Rather, it has to mean: "Whoever enters on the way is on the path to the realization of the Christ-Self."

But in order to be on the way I have to start out on that way. It is that movement that matters. Sitting idly around by the street sign is not being on the way, even if I think the name on the sign is the only right one. It is not about the name of the street. Whoever gets up and goes is on the way. Whoever seeks the truth finds me—that is, the Christ-reality in her inmost being; and whoever finds that, finds life to the full.

*I want to pick up on that word "movement." Once before we spoke about how—to the extent that we persist in remaining in an immature stage—we are led by our ego. That ego is fragile and therefore has to assert itself constantly because it is afraid that at bottom it is nothing. How can we overcome that stage of immaturity? It seems as if the means that is strong enough to transform people is pain, suffering. When we set Jesus and Buddha alongside one another and compare them, we see a number of similarities in the way they think about human transformation. Empathy or representative suffering seems a central path to salvation for both of them. In your experience, what characterizes this Jesus Christ and how is his teaching different from that of the Buddha?*

### Anselm Grün

The theme of suffering is very important for the Buddha, but he sees greed and being bound to the world as the fundamental cause of all suffering. To the extent that I withdraw from the world and free myself, I will also be free from suffering. C. G. Jung once held a famous conversation with an evangelical theologian. Jung had been in India, and he noted that in the East people try to get free of suffering by withdrawing from the world; in the West they try to deaden suffering with activism and drugs. But the path leads through suffering, says Jung, and he pointed to the cross. Jesus passed through suffering. So there are similarities. One can learn a lot from Buddhism—in particular, inner freedom from the world. But the Buddha dies smiling, while Jesus died screaming on the cross. For me, Jesus is also the hope for the poor sucker who may not follow the spiritual path but stays stuck in her suffering. That is a difference: not withdrawing from suffering but going through suffering and transforming it. Of course, it is more congenial that the Buddha dies smiling, but for me it is a little elitist. Is that really a path for everyone, even those who are stuck in their suffering? Johann Baptist Metz,[32] who is no conservative theologian, says: the memory of suffering contributes in important ways to a sensitivity to suffering in our world. If we become desensitized to suffering, our lives will be brutalized. Empathy and mercy are the same for Jesus and Buddha. We can certainly learn from them to have empathy not only with other people but also with Nature, with creation, with everything.

### David Steindl-Rast

From my point of view it is a great contribution of the Christian tradition that it does not set suffering over against God, according to the motto: I have been abandoned by God, or I'm being punished by him, therefore I have to suffer. Instead, it shows that suffering is part of life and life is the expression of the Mystery we call God. In that way suffering is divinized by the Christian tradition, just as are joy and all of life. Suffering is part of life and of being alive.

The Christian tradition brings that as its gift to the world's other traditions. In India I had the opportunity a number of times to see little altars in private dwellings. There, among all the many statues and pictures of gods, you again and again find that really corny picture of Jesus kneeling in prayer on the Mount of Olives, the moon shining through the clouds. The painting is frequently reproduced here too. Believing Hindus say: that is the suffering God. He is important to them.

Another experience of mine points the same way: when the Dalai Lama traveled to the United States for the first time, he was not yet surrounded by such huge crowds. Once I was able to sit with him in a small group. I was the only Christian there. Then someone who had a very critical attitude toward the Christian tradition said to the Dalai Lama: "Your Holiness, for two thousand years the Christians have been wallowing in their suffering, while the Buddhists have a marvelous way of overcoming it. What would you say about that?" The Dalai Lama answered: "Careful; it is not that simple. In Buddhism, suffering is not overcome by leaving pain behind. Suffering is overcome by bearing the pains of others." That is the ideal of the Bodhisattva, and it is no different from the Christian ideal.

### Anselm Grün

When you enter into a real religious dialogue you find many similarities. But I haven't seen it that way when it comes to the topic of suffering. Certainly there is a masochistic wallowing in suffering, but for me the central thing about the death and resurrection of Jesus is the exercise of transforming what attacks me from outside into an act of love. My mother said it very simply. At the end of her life she was ill but always happy. I asked her: How do you do it? She said: It's nothing. I offer it up for my children and grandchildren. In the '60s, offering things up had a very negative tone. She had no other language for it, but she transformed the illness that attacked her into an act of surrender on behalf of others. Her grandchildren loved to be with her. There are other sick people who constantly complain and almost give healthy people a bad conscience when they visit. Hers was the art, not of suppressing pain, but of transforming it into an act of love. If the Dalai Lama said something similar, I see that as a major agreement.

### David Steindl-Rast

In comparing traditions one must always match the best with the best and the worst with the worst. Wallowing in suffering is the worst in Christianity and one of its blind alleys. But it is not typical. I love it that you speak of your mother. In the Bible, both the Hebrew and the Greek, suffering is often associated with the image of birth pangs. Suffering is seen as a process of being born to greater and deeper life. That surrender begins already at birth. In order to bring a child into the world, the mother must suffer.

*Brother David, I want to ask you again: Is it a historical accident that you chose a Christian path of following Jesus? Or would you say today: It's all the same; I could also have been a Buddhist, and that would be okay too? My question has to do with a choice, because you are very familiar with both worlds—the Christian and the Buddhist.*

### David Steindl-Rast

If I had been born into and brought up in a Buddhist world, I might have known nothing of Christianity and I would probably have become a Buddhist monk, because a monk is what I wanted to be. But I grew up in Christianity, and I am glad and thankful for it. I once had a dialogue with Baker Roshi,[33] and he said to me, "Now for once, set aside all your Christian convictions. During our conversation, imagine that they are all false, so that we can play ball on a level playing field." So I tried to imagine that. It didn't work out very well. I tried harder and harder to imagine that my Christian convictions are false, but in the end I had to admit: "I'm sorry. I simply can't do it. I can't jump over my own shadow. I am a Christian, and I identify totally with that." But that only means that I express my humanity in a Christian way. What we are really talking about is not the Christian or the Buddhist thing but the human. I believe that the greatest glory of Christianity is that it really leads to what is human. The greatest glory of Buddhism is that it also leads to what is human. The human is greater and more important than the form in which we express it. I think you see it somewhat in the same way, but probably you would say it differently?

### Anselm Grün

I value the dialogue with Buddhism, but I, too, am totally a Christian. As Christians we must not see the absolute claim in a fundamentalist way, but I am convinced that of all the ways, the Christian way of Jesus—not the one we have always preached in history—is the most humane. Sometimes we only begin to recognize who this Jesus is in our dialogue with Buddhism and Hinduism, because it opens our eyes to sides of Jesus we have overlooked in Western theology. This Jesus is, first and last, the challenge to

me because he is God's self-communication. We can understand him more deeply when we dive into the essence of
the other religions.

*Christian faith is not the religion of the "winners." It is not a reli-
gion that believes one can automatically gain salvation by keeping
particular rules of conduct, nor does it believe that by immersing
oneself more and more deeply in esoteric mysteries one can gain
insight into higher realities that are essentially closed to ordinary
people. On the contrary, Christianity teaches that every person is
dependent on understanding and forgiveness and the grace of God.
The Jewish-Christian tradition as a whole, and Jesus, most par-
ticularly, shows that it is essential to stand on the side of the poor,
to aid the hungry, to care for the sick, to visit prisoners, to seek out
and accompany the lost. Why is this sympathy for the victims so
central for Jesus?*

### Anselm Grün

C. G. Jung once said that the greatest enemy of transformation is a successful life. There is, however, also a Christian
"theology of success" in the United States: only one who
is successful is a real Christian. That is another danger. We
shouldn't see success as something negative, but Jesus cared
for sinners because they were open and had sensed that they
had to repent. That is to say, there is a kind of self-righteousness
in which one closes oneself against God and, therefore,
also against other people. One holds oneself to be correct
and "okay." One justifies oneself and goes on living that
way. That was a horror for Jesus. He seeks people who are
open, who are truthful. Those who are truthful, who are
genuine, also know their shadow sides, their mistakes, and
their weaknesses. Certainly there have also been excesses

in Christianity that heavily emphasized the idea: "You are bad. You are a sinner." That falsifies Jesus' message. Jesus does not say, "You are a sinner." He turns toward sinners and trusts them to be able to straighten up. Jesus' concern shows who God is. God pays attention to everyone, not only the successful. That is an image of hope for everyone.

### David Steindl-Rast

I agree completely. In this connection I am thinking about Jesus' baptism. In Mark's gospel—historically the oldest gospel—it simply says that crowds of people were going to John to be baptized and that Jesus also went to be baptized (Mark 1:9-11). Nothing more. In Matthew's gospel, John the Baptizer refuses Jesus and tells him that he himself really ought to be baptized by Jesus (Matt 3:1-17). That appears to be a later development. However that may be, Jesus let himself be baptized. If Jesus is really a human being he participates in the sinfulness of the world, even if he personally did not sin. It is part of the human condition that each of us participates in its brokenness, its separation from the divine. Jesus, as a human person, fully accepted that and showed it by letting himself be baptized. Unfortunately, that is not often preached because most preachers start with the passage in Matthew and not the one in Mark.

### Anselm Grün

Or think of Jesus' temptation in the wilderness. We have often interpreted Jesus as God's Son in a mythological way, as if he were only God. He was entirely a human being, and so he was also subject to temptation. It is religiously gifted people in particular who are tempted to misuse religion, to put themselves above other people and consider themselves something special. Jesus refuses, in the temptation story (Luke 4:1-13), to want to be something special. He is wholly human and, nevertheless, he does miracles. He doesn't want to be the guru everyone submissively follows.

### David Steindl-Rast

He even goes one step further. When someone addresses him as "good master," he asks, "Why do you call me good? No one is good but God alone" (Luke 18:19). That is certainly a Jesus saying, because the evangelist would not have had him say anything like that.

# Saint, Sinner, and Called Out, or:

## The Church(es) between Being and Seeming to Be

*Worldwide, most people are religious. But if we look more closely, we see that in Christianity, and also in other religions, there is a growing dissatisfaction with religious institutions. People have become more skeptical. That may have something to do with the fact that organized religion has created a kind of "fast food faith" and relies less on authentic experience of God and more on a "religious insurance system." Then religious life consists in fulfilling particular obligations and rules of behavior in order to be part of a supposedly "superior, redeemed group." What, in contrast, is the sign of an authentic Christian life? What should the church, as the community of believers, really be?*

### Anselm Grün

The church should, for one thing, be a place of spiritual encounter where people can have their own personal experience of God. The church should be a place where people who have been damaged and wounded in this world feel themselves accepted. Of course, the church, like every institution, is also subject to the temptation to power. It was in danger of creating fear and threatening people that they would not get to heaven. Or it fell victim to the other danger, namely, of expanding human grandiosity and narcissism by telling them: when you pray you are something special and not as lost as the others. That is also a danger to which many fall victim when they think nothing can happen to them if they go to church. Those are, instead, images that strengthen infantilism and narcissism rather than transforming them. The church's way of faith is a path on which I encounter God with my whole truth and my shadow side, show all that to God, and sense that God can transform all of it. For me that is what is crucial, and not that I put myself above others. The danger that threatens many fundamentalists is the attitude that "we are something better," we put ourselves above others and demean them. But that has nothing to do with transformation.

*My philosophy professor, Augustinus Karl Wucherer-Huldenfeld,*[34] *once said: "The great problem begins when the worshipers of the only true God become the only true worshipers of God." At the moment when I make myself or my group the absolute, disaster befalls my religion.*

### David Steindl-Rast

I want to say something on the subject of why the majority of humans are religious and yet are turning more and more against religion. The question itself implies a difference between religiosity and the religions. We can say that every human person is religious, because it is part of the nature of the human to be confronted by the mystery of life. The religions are expressions of this religiosity, developed in doctrine, morality, and ritual. Religiosity also leads unavoidably to community. The experience of community is of the essence of religiosity, not only internally with the divine Mystery but also externally with other people. But when a community becomes larger and less manageable it requires organization and becomes an institution. Then the problem begins. Most people have no problem with religiosity; their problem is with religious institutions. We have to be aware that every institution, whether it acts in the academic, medical, or political sphere, was founded for a particular purpose. It very quickly forgets the purpose and its whole energy is devoted to self-formation, self-affirmation, and self-expansion. All religious institutions have fallen into that trap. Still, most of them have the advantage that they transmit truth. I still have great respect for the church, not because it is an institution, but because it is the mediator of a message.

I compare tradition to a water main: the church suffers from the syndrome of rusty piping. If we could look into our subterranean water systems we would never drink water again. And yet they bring us clean water, even when they are rusty.

We can look at institutions the same way and then use the strength we draw from the pure water to realize the life-giving message again and again in small communities. That is why one becomes a monk. One lives in a small community that tries to realize what the institution originally wanted but that as such it cannot bring to fruition.

**Anselm Grün**

All three aspects you have named—doctrine, morality, and ritual—have something positive and healthy about them. Doctrine exists to protect human freedom and dignity. It exists so that people can see rightly. We can observe that in the negative when, for example, the Third Reich was able to mislead people with false imagery. But the danger is that doctrine will become dogmatism and not speak rightly about humanity. Ethics and morality are also part of the human, but they are different from moralizing. Today we have to seek globally for common ethical values, as Hans Küng suggested in his "World-Ethos" project.[35] And the third thing is ritual: rituals are healthy, but they too can be misused or harden into ritualism. Rituals are something healthy for the soul, as C. G. Jung so often described. But just as everything can be misused, so also rituals are misused by totalitarian states. That is why I trust that in the church, despite the rusty pipes, there will always be breakthroughs. Church history is full of scandals but, thank God, it is full of healthy eruptions as well.

### David Steindl-Rast

I have a picture of these deviations in teaching and morality you speak of: At the beginning there is the message of salvation, the Good News. It bubbles up freshly, springs up like a fountain of clear water. But the climate in our world is very cold, and everything freezes. Then dogma becomes dogmatism, morality becomes moralism, and ritual becomes ritualism. All those "isms" are frozen living water. The question is how we can liquefy the ice into living water again. My answer is: with the warmth of our own hearts. We have to melt the ice with our experience and our aliveness. The heart of every religion is the religion of the heart.

# In Dialogue with the Mystery, or:

## The "Our Father" and God's Trustworthiness

One of the central prayers of Christianity, if not the most important, is the "Our Father." Jesus used it to teach his disciples how to pray to God the Father. What can we learn from this prayer about the dialogue of humans with God?

### Anselm Grün

The first words, "*Our* Father," already indicate that we cannot speak to God as separate individuals. We are in community, and God is the God of us all. We may not use God for our own purposes. Next comes that God's name is to be "hallowed." God's name is also hallowed in that our life succeeds. Irenaeus says, "*Gloria Dei homo vivens*: the glory of God is the human being fully alive."[36]

Then come the human petitions for food, both earthly and spiritual. "Forgive us our trespasses as we forgive those who trespass against us" means: we cannot pray to God without clarifying our relationships. For me personally it is also important that I call to mind in this prayer that my father, mother, and grandparents also prayed it. They did not always know what they were praying, but it enabled them to take charge of their lives. When I pray it, I share in the strength of their lives and their faith. So I am bound into a tradition going back to Jesus. This rootedness in a long tradition of people who pray is important to me, just as it is also important that I constantly test my image of God against the Our Father.

### David Steindl-Rast

That tradition is important to me, too, when I remember how my grandmother taught us the Our Father. You see it rightly: it is prayer itself that warms what is frozen and hard into living water. Because what I meant by the warmth of the heart is relationship—to myself, to others, and to God. That relationship is expressed in prayer. "Our Father" itself already speaks of relationship: the Father, the community, and I who pray this prayer belong inseparably together. It helped me personally a great deal to understand that the fundamental ideas in the Our Father go back to Jesus, though certainly not in this form. It has a highly complex artistic form, a chiastic structure. At the time when the Our Father received its current form, children learned the alphabet not only from A to Z but also from Z to A. The letter M was important because it was in the center. People had this chiastic form in their heads. I see this prayer that way too.

Between "Our Father," the address, and "give us our daily bread," there is an axis. We stand as children before the Father who gives us daily bread, that is, everything we need. That, so to speak, is the central axis of the Our Father. On the one side, then, is the descending branch with three petitions, and on the other side is the ascending branch with three petitions. "Hallowed be Thy Name"—that says it all. "Through you His Name is dishonored among the nations," the prophets lament, and they mean that we are not living as children of God. If we live as children of God, we honor God's name. Another way of saying it is "your kingdom come": when we honor God's name, God's reign is already in our midst. "Thy will be done"—the reign of God is the will of God.

Hallowing God's name also means having reverence for what God's name stands for. It means advocating reverently for what God advocates. The bread petition is the center and turning point of the Our Father. It summarizes everything: as children of God we ask the Father for everything we need.

The next three petitions then stand parallel in reverse order, thus "chiastically" to the corresponding first three. First comes the petition for forgiveness of our trespasses, "as we also forgive those who trespass against us." That is parallel to "thy will be done, on earth as it is in heaven." We fulfill God's will when we forgive on earth as God forgives in heaven. Then comes a parallel to "thy kingdom come," namely, "and lead us not into temptation." The greatest and most dangerous temptation is to fall away from God's reign and become worldly, that is, to fall victim to the world of the ego, of greed, of envy, and of violence. The contrary is the reign of God, which is characterized by mutual respect, sharing, and peace.

The last petition, then, is: "deliver us from evil," which is parallel to "hallowed be Thy name." Evil is what is contrary to the name of God, what contradicts God's will, the reign of God. And so the circle of the seven petitions of the Our Father is closed. The "amen" is also a very important part of the prayer, because it summarizes our trust in God. In Hebrew, God's trustworthiness is called *amunah*. We respond to that trustworthiness with our trust, and we say, "Amen." I pray the Our Father many times a day. It is very important to me. It inculcates in me, again and again, the father-son image for my relationship to the divine Mystery. And that image was determinative for Jesus' own piety.

# Three and One? or:

## A Brief User's Guide to the Trinity

*At the center of Christian doctrine is belief in the triune God. At first glance that looks like an unbelievably complex academic-theological construct. Many people say: but we believe in one God. Why then three persons? The doctrine of the Trinity is probably not understood by the majority of Christians, and most certainly in dialogue with other religions the Trinity is again and again a source of misunderstanding and causes heads to shake. What exactly is the doctrine of the triune God all about? And how can we understand it in very practical terms?*

### Anselm Grün

For me, God-image and Self-image coincide in the Trinity. The image of the triune God is that of the God who is open to human beings. That is: I cannot speak of human beings without at the same time speaking of God, because God is also in me through the Holy Spirit. There is only one God, but this God encounters us as the Creator, the Father; as the Son who accompanies us and is in us as the true Self; and as Holy Spirit, who urges us on and fills us with love. That is the God who reaches into our hearts, not some distant God who is enthroned above the heavens and gives us orders. The fight over the dogma of the Trinity was really a fight about humanity. What is the mystery of humanity?

To speak rightly about God is to speak rightly of the human being, who is plunged into God. His/her spirit is God's spirit. Her/his Self is Christ's Self but also the God before whom we fall down in reverence and to whom we pray as Creator. Thus, Trinity means the different ways in which God is in relationship with us, and we are in relationship with God: the God who is outside and different, the God who is with us, and the God who permeates us.

### David Steindl-Rast

This being fully embedded in God and God's presence in us is for me also the most important thing about believing in a triune God. I like to use the image of a vessel that is completely full of seawater and submerged in the sea. That is how we are filled and surrounded by God. Every image has its limits, but we need images. There is a major difficulty in the doctrine of the Trinity by virtue of the fact that we have to talk about "persons." When we speak of three divine persons, we are not using the common notion of person with which we are familiar. Even early in the history of the dogma's origins that led to justified criticism within the church.

### Anselm Grün

In Greek it is also called *hypostasis*.[37]

**David Steindl-Rast**

Yes, and nowadays "person" is a misleading translation of *hypostasis*. I would prefer to speak of ways of appearing, that is, the ways God appears to us. If we go back to the mystery that is known to us through the reality we call life, we can distinguish three aspects: first, the source of life, from which life constantly streams and emerges in every instant from possibility into reality. This origin from which everything springs forth we call Father. Second, the living reality that comes from the source we call Son. And third—because otherwise all that would remain static—comes the aliveness. This divine aliveness is what we mean when we speak of the Holy Spirit.

**Anselm Grün**

Origin and source, form, spirit, and dynamic—we can speak of it that way. The church fathers and philosophers tried to see humanity itself as threefold. Plato divides the human into body, spirit, and soul; Augustine into understanding, will, and *memoria*, the ability to remember. They always saw the parallels to God. To that extent it is legitimate to speak as you do about "life" and so to bring God and the human together.

**David Steindl-Rast**

Augustine gives us the lovely comparison of Father, Logos, and Holy Spirit to silence, word, and understanding. From silence comes the word. Everything that is, is word, and it proceeds by way of understanding back into silence. Understanding is the process by which we listen to a word in such a way that it seizes us and leads us to the place from which it comes.

### Anselm Grün

Understanding is the Holy Spirit. The word is the Son. And the origin of the word, the Father, speaks out of silence. Those are images that can give us a glimpse of the Mystery. Dogmatics does not nail things down. It doesn't know everything exactly. Through its paradoxical language it causes something we can only guess at to ring true.

### David Steindl-Rast

That is why the Cappadocian fathers[38] also speak of the ring-dance of the Trinity. The leader of the ring is the Logos, who comes forth from silence. The dancing is the Holy Spirit. In the Holy Spirit we dance back to the origin, the Father. I find that image very inspiring and beautiful.

*You, Father Anselm, previously began to explain the Trinity with the argument that when we speak of God we are always at the same time saying something about the human. Let me take up that thread again. If we consider human life in light of this triune God, our Christian life should be a trinitarian life. Is that so?*

**Anselm Grün**

To speak in trinitarian fashion of human beings means that all three spheres of the human are saturated with God, that God is not only in our spirit but also in body and soul. That means: open God and open human. The two are intertwined.

*Where I wanted to go with it was this: being human is not an individual matter. Being human is always being-in-relationship. I become a human being through you. Without the you—in the form of my parents—I would never even have come into the world, and they in turn not without a you. Between "I" and you, or you and you, there is always a third dimension: the level of relationship that represents the real power between the two. So this triune dimension exists not only in every relationship but also in every human creative act—or how do you see it?*

**Anselm Grün**

This level of relationship is very important. Martin Buber put great emphasis on that as well. The essence of Christianity is that it is a religion of relationship. It is about the relationship to God and to other human beings. The personal encounter with the You, between "I" and you—there is love in that. Love is the Holy Spirit. The other religions also know of relationship, but one must say that the tendency in Buddhism is to be directed more to the individual, and the level of relationship is not so well developed. That is not meant to be a valuation. It does not mean that Christians are better at relationships. There are some marvelous Buddhist people who emanate a great deal of relationship, but that is not the focus of their religion.

**David Steindl-Rast**

Dogmatically, we also say that the one thing in which the divine persons are different is in their relationship to one another. God is one God, and relationship is part of that Mystery. God is relationship in God's innermost nature. That is also one way of expressing the triune. We have discovered this divine relationship. We can also say that it has been revealed to us because, after all, everything is gift.

# How Can I Live, Ultimately? or:

## On the Mortal and the Eternal

*From the moment of our birth we are mortal. Death is our ultimate possibility. That is, in everything we do and don't do we are moving inevitably toward death, to a boundary we cannot influence. We are afraid of death because we are afraid of nothingness. We see that those who have gone before us dwindle into dust. But we can't see beyond that. That makes us afraid. And for that reason we often repress death. Many people struggle over and over again, with useless means, to avoid death, according to the motto: "Let us today eat and drink because tomorrow we die!" (1 Cor 15:32). Does faith help us to deal with death not only more serenely—without greed, without stress—but also without repressing it?*

### Anselm Grün

To begin with, the thought of death is an invitation to live deliberately, to live in the moment. There are fairy tales in which death is overcome, but then it gets boring because we discover that life without death has no excitement. Our limitedness invites us to pay attention or—as Jesus says—to live alertly. Faith can help us to understand that death is not something terrible, because I will die into God and be complete. C. G. Jung once said: after midlife only those who are ready to die, to let go, remain alive. He means that those who refuse to struggle in the first half of life are the same as those who in the second half of life cannot let go. My experience is that many people are afraid of death because they have not lived. Unlived life is hard to let go. Those who live deliberately can also let go. Fear of death has various aspects. For the most part it is fear of loss of control: that something will come along that I cannot master. For many it is fear of the unknown. What happens after death? Is there anything? Then faith is a promise, as Jesus says: "Today you will be with me in Paradise" (Luke 23:43). Of course we may also fail, but we have hope that we will die into God, leave ourselves to God, and be perfected. How that happens we do not know. We can trust the biblical images and at the same time know that what awaits us is beyond all images. How it really is—that is something no one can say.

### David Steindl-Rast

Maybe we can expand this understanding by going back to the difference between I and Self. Our Self is not in space and time; we experience it in a now that is beyond space and time. Our "I," on the other hand, exists in space and time. It is both the greatness and the task of the human to live in this double sphere. Though they are one, the I and the Self undergo two different processes. For my "I," the length of my life from conception to death represents a process that is about development—similar to the process from seed to bloom to fruit, which in turn is a new seed. For the Self it is not about development but about a different process we might call enrichment. This is the sense in which I understand what the poet Rilke says of us: "We are the bees of the invisible. We wildly collect the honey of the visible, to store it in the great golden hive of the invisible."[39] I see the meaning of all the joy and suffering we experience in time as an enrichment, a bringing of it all into this "golden hive" of what is beyond time. Beyond time, the Self is enriched by all the sufferings and joys we undergo during our time on earth. In this double sphere, you might say, we stand on two legs, on the one side with our "I" in space and time, on the other with our Self in the Now, in the timeless Enduring. I see my task, at my great age, to be making the Self increasingly the leg on which I stand, until my "I" is only my free leg. When my ego dies and is no longer there, any more than it was there before I existed, the Self remains—and, taken up into the Self, every moment of my time with all its fullness. Certainly I cannot picture that for myself. An embryo cannot imagine, either, how someone can live outside the mother's womb, and a caterpillar cannot imagine what it means to fly as a butterfly.

> *That makes me want to ask: does it make any sense to hold fast to an individual humanity, or does the individuality of the human being transcend into a common Self in which it is dissolved like chocolate in milk?*

### David Steindl-Rast

As a Christian, I believe in the resurrection of the flesh. Therefore I try to understand what it can all mean, this enrichment and "bringing home to the great golden honeycomb." I know a lot of people who say, "I am living a full life, and when it is over, it is over." They don't live badly, either—or do you have a different experience?

**Anselm Grün**

C. G. Jung once said: "As a psychologist I cannot say whether there is life after death. But as a psychologist I know about the wisdom of the soul. The soul knows that everything does not end with death, however one may imagine that. As a psychologist I also know that I am restless and unsettled when I live contrary to the wisdom of the soul." To that extent Jung sees, as a psychologist, that it is good to believe. We should not judge.

There are Christians who die in fear, and there are others who die calmly because they can let go, because they trust that they are somehow sustained. But back to the question: resurrection of the flesh means resurrection of the person. My love happens through the body. My body is the storehouse of my experiences. What has ripened uniquely, that comes to God, but at the same time it becomes one with God. The individual and the becoming-one have to be seen together.

I refuse to say, as my fellow Benedictine Willigis Jäger[40] does: "The soul dissolves like a wave in the sea"—that is, the "I" is completely dissolved in God. Then nothing is important any more. The person is saved and is one in God. We speak of reuniting, but we should not think of it as if it were a class reunion. It escapes our grasp. But I want to maintain the tension between the person and the unity.

**David Steindl-Rast**

If I have understood you correctly: because in our whole nature we are related to a "You" above all time and space, that cannot change when our time is at its end. The relationship endures. It has eternal existence. It can probably not be proven that what we have experienced physically survives even after death, but I have an argument for it: when the immortal Divine is present to us even now, in our experience of every chestnut blossom, every eyelash of a beloved person, even the smallest sigh, how can that experience suddenly vanish in death?

So I rejoice to think of meeting my mother again, my grandmother, and my friends who have died. But I also want to see people I could never meet in person. Joseph von Eichendorff,[41] for example—I would really love to get to know him. I want to ski with Eichendorff, because he never skied in his lifetime. He would certainly enjoy it. I can easily imagine it—and do I not have the right to imagine? "What might have been and what has been," says T. S. Eliot, "point to one end, which is always present."[42]

### Anselm Grün

I can also imagine meeting Augustine or Teresa of Avila.[43] We can trust the images. If we think it through logically and see billions of human beings, it's difficult. At the same time it is beyond space and time, and there everything is possible. How exact it is, we cannot know. We can only talk about it in pictures, but the reality is always beyond all picturing. The images make it live. So the Bible also speaks of a "banquet" and "drinking wine."

*When we ask about mortality we are asking about the meaning of time and how time and eternity relate to one another. There is an amazing phenomenon that is usually overlooked but is perceptible*

*in our conversation: there is time! Now and now and now. . . .*
*Our meeting here, our thoughts and words were never before here*
*as they are now, this minute. So something comes to be out of . . .*
*nothing. But that is an incredible thing; it takes your breath away.*
*Really, it is a miracle. So: what does time teach us about ourselves*
*and about eternity?*

### Anselm Grün

For years I have done New Year's Eve programs. At about
midnight we would be in the church. From ten minutes
before twelve to ten minutes after twelve there was silence.
I gave a brief introduction: The old time is running out and
the new, unused time is coming. We know these phenomena: How at one point time seems very long, and in an
intensive experience time runs faster. Then there are also
experiences in prayer and in contemplation in which time
and eternity meld into the pure present. Meister Eckhart[44]
speaks of the "fullness of time." That is pure present. It is
timeless. The Greek distinguished between time as *chronos*
(the time that passes and devours us) and *kairos* (the time
of the proper moment or of fullness).

The Greeks imagined Kairos as a youth with a curl on
his forehead. When Kairos comes along one has to grab
him by it. Of course, there are also missed opportunities,
but every time has its own. They are not the same as those
of yesterday; they are different. The opportunity for the
Berlin Wall to come down was there at that time. Today
there are others, but it is also important to be able to enjoy
time without a purpose—without having something to do.
Time is simply there.

### David Steindl-Rast

Time has many different aspects. For science, time is a function of space. That refers to the aspect of time we can measure with a clock—Chronos, as you have named it from Greek mythology. That is not what interests us here. We have the right to focus on other aspects of time as well, aspects that touch us personally. You pointed to a very important one with the image of Kairos, the youth with the curly lock on his forehead. For me the most important aspect of time is the opportunity we have to grab it by the forelock. The fact that every moment gives me an opportunity is a gift. By making something of the opportunity that is given, I show that I am grateful for it.

Through this give-and-take, all of life becomes a dialogue with the unfathomable Mystery that gives me opportunities at every moment. Eternity, out of which time bubbles up, intends that we make something of it. Now and now and now gratefully making something of every opportunity given, then, means entering in the midst of time into a dialogue with eternity.

# Being Entirely My Self, or:

## *Prayer as a Space of Freedom*

*Prayer and religious meditation are primal human actions. We find them in all cultures and religions, and prayer may possibly be as old as humanity itself. Prayer belongs to being human. Yet there are particular forms of prayer that can lead us astray. For example, there is the temptation to try to convince God of something, to summon God, to manipulate God with magic and force God to do this or that. How can such wrong ideas and attitudes be avoided? What is the meaning of prayer and contemplative life in the true sense?*

### Anselm Grün

Petition is just one form of prayer. We may ask God for anything, but at the end of every petition stands: thy will be done. But we may express our neediness before God, and when we do that, it is transformed. Still, prayer is more than petition. Prayer is an encounter with God. I hold myself out to God and can "let it all out." For me, prayer is like a therapeutic self-knowledge before the face of God. Prayer can also be nothing more than simple, silent sitting before God and waiting for what comes up within me. I hold that out to God and hope that God's love pours into the whole of it. Everything may be, and everything will be transformed.

Sometimes I invite people to pray to God out loud for half an hour—and I do it myself. What do I really want to say to God? When I hear myself, I notice first of all that this is just verbiage, not the truth. It is not what I want to say to God. It is only superficial routine. So, as I speak, I gradually arrive at my deeper truth and longing. When I express what I long for in the depth of my heart, then something very intimate happens through prayer.

### David Steindl-Rast

That seems to me like a very interesting exercise—I've never tried it. Confusing petition with prayer has something to do with the fact that the words are related in our language.[45] I remember a mother who reminded her little son to say his good-night prayer. He said to her: "Mama, you know, there are nights when I don't need anything." A lot of people think that way. They only start to pray when they need something.

You also addressed the difference between religion and magic, prayer and conjuring. I think that genuine prayer not only ends but also begins with "thy will be done." Magical conjuring has something else in mind: "my will be done." Magic is most effective if one knows the name of a god. We think of it that way because a teacher has to call a student by name in order to be listened to. "You, third from the left at the back"—that makes little impression. I also feel safer with a dog if I can call out "Flocky!" than if I can only say, "You, dog, leave me alone!"

The name is very important as the means for getting control of someone, and magic is intended to get control of the divine reality and make it useful. That is why God says to Moses: "I will not tell you my name." Even the word

"Yʜᴡʜ," often translated "I am who I am," is not a name in the real sense of the word. It means: "I will be present in the way I choose to be present." I will encounter you, but not as you want to force me to. And the first petition in the Our Father, "hallowed be thy name," is a petition that we not slip into magic but instead give God the freedom to surprise us.

### Anselm Grün

What you have said about the name of God—"I will be there as who I want to be there"—is one thing. We could also say: "I am I," or "I am unique." That is one aspect of God. The Greeks translated it *egō eimi ho ōn*—"I am the One Who Is." We could also say that is incorrect, but for me that, too, is a deep experience of God: when I am simply original, only pure Being—without having to prove myself, justify myself, or defend myself. Sometimes we have such an experience: I am simple. Then we get a hint of God, who is pure Being, who doesn't have to prove or do anything in order to be. In that way this experience of "I am" can also lead to an experience of God's being.

### David Steindl-Rast

Yes, Buber also places great emphasis on the "I," which essentially exists in relation to the "Thou." It is always about "being-in-relationship." Being alive means actualizing relationship. Prayer is fundamentally a being alive through relationship to God. The glory of God is the living human being[46]—in the sense of a conscious being alive through being oriented toward God.

We experience our relationship to that ultimate Mystery we point to with the word "God" in three very different ways. First, there is the realm of silence. When we allow ourselves to sink into silence we experience a whole world of prayer: the prayer of stillness, our prayer to the Father. The Father is the gulf of stillness out of which comes the Logos, the Word. Living out of the Word of God is a second avenue to encounter with God. It, too, opens for us a whole world of prayer: listening to the word that God speaks to me in this given moment and responding; discovering that I myself am a word of God. I am a word God speaks into the world, but I am not only spoken by God; I am also addressed by God. Ferdinand Ebner has worked that out very insightfully in his writings.[47]

Then there is a third way to experience the divine Mystery, a third world of prayer: that of understanding. We understand most completely by doing. Every teacher knows that if you say it to the pupils it will go in one ear and out the other. Show it to them, and there is more hope that they will remember it. Have them do it, and they will understand it from within. The prayer of understanding is called *contemplatio in actione*:[48] God is grasped in doing. Rilke also said that very beautifully: "You're captured only through the deed," he prays, for he knows that

> Basically only prayer exists;
> our hands have been anointed for this
> and nothing they made did not supplicate;
> whether one painted or mowed,
> from the striving of each tool
> did piety evolve.[49]

Everything is prayer, either in silence, in word, or in understanding through doing. That is complete immersion in the triune God through prayer. Prayer means synchronizing yourself with life through silence, word, and understanding—with life, understood as the image of the divine Mystery.

### Anselm Grün

It is also important for me that prayer is, for one thing, the silence in which everything comes to the fore, dialogical prayer in which I show God everything, and yet the goal of prayer is to achieve a stillness in which all thoughts cease, in which I am one with God. The early monks say the same thing: the dignity of the human is to pray without distraction. That means being one with God.

For me, prayer means getting into the space where God rules in me. There I have a right to live. There no enemy can threaten me. There I am sheltered. Prayer is a refuge, a space of freedom where no one can injure me, where people's opinion doesn't count, where no guilt feelings oppress me, but I am entirely myself. That, for me, is the goal of prayer.

*Both of you are members of the most ancient Western order, the Benedictines.*[50] *Saint Benedict centered contemplation in a special way:* ora et labora et lege—*pray, work, and read. What can we learn from the monastic-contemplative life?*

### Anselm Grün

The guests who come to the monastery are touched most deeply by the rhythm of prayer and work. They can also find a good rhythm between action and contemplation in their own lives without having to copy us or pray as much as we do. For example, they can begin and end the day in a spiritual rhythm. Rhythm has to do with rituals. A ritual is a holy time, a time of withdrawal from the world. They can take care to create a sacred time in the middle of the day, a time that belongs entirely to themselves, apart from all the hectic: a time to breathe out, to live as oneself instead of being lived. The other aspect of *ora* is *labora*, understanding by doing. For work can certainly be a spiritual challenge. When surrender happens in prayer, it should be that way in work as well. Many people complain that they can't get around to prayer because they have too much work to do. So we need not only ritual and time but also a kind of peacefulness in work.

It is central to Benedict's *ora et labora* that prayer and work are linked, that work is also a place in which I learn to surrender myself, to serve, to let go of my ego. For Benedict there is no contradiction between work and prayer. That is why he says that if someone is standing around idle on Sunday he ought to get to work. So it is a matter of surrendering oneself to God in prayer and in work. I also know people who see prayer and contemplation as a narcissistic circling around oneself. There was someone who once wanted to enter the monastery; he said: "I am a contemplative type. I can only work three hours at the most." But he would never make it—even with the Trappists.[51] They work at least six hours. Some people have a lot of time for themselves, but it doesn't flow by them because they are always focused on themselves. But prayer is a flow just as work should be.

*Do you see giving oneself to work as a form of contemplative life too, in the sense that one need not be thinking of anything religious, but that everything depends on how I devote myself to something, whether I am plowing a field, making a cupboard, caring for other people, designing a building, or writing a book? Whatever it is: if I am entirely present to the thing and enter into it, is it contemplation, or is there a difference?*

## Anselm Grün

Surrender is the right word. I give myself up to plowing, building, or writing. I am entirely immersed in it. Those who are on a narcissistic prayer path just circle around themselves; they are not at work but prefer always to be somewhere else, preferably by themselves. But then they get stuck and do not get into the flow of things. The question is: What emotions do I spread through my works? Do I diffuse peace, love? In that sense we need to constantly purify our emotions in work through prayer. I was cellarer[52] for a long time, and in that job there is often annoyance and disappointment. But I saw clearly that it is up to me how I go into the office the next day. Do I show my annoyance to those who have disappointed me, or do peace, concern, clarity, and ultimately love stream out of me? Work is the test whether what I pray is true or not. It is a test and at the same time a continuation of prayer. It is about surrender and freedom from the ego. You can always tell the people who are intent only on proving themselves in their work by how tense they are. The farmer who is entirely absorbed in plowing is calm and selfless.

## David Steindl-Rast

There is a monk in everyone. In every individual there dwells a longing for the One. *Monachōs*[53] means the one. Human longing seeks to find the One within multiplicity. That is then realized in monastic life in a very particular way, but in many traditions we find stories about a monk who thinks he has climbed the highest rung of the ladder of ascesis and then is told by an angel that he still needs a teacher—and to the monk's astonishment, that great master is a very odd layperson: a tavernkeeper, for example, or in Buddhism, a butcher. Stories like that are meant to show that nonmonks often accomplish in secret everything the monk strives for. Father Damasus Winzen, the founder of our monastery in the United States, always told us monks: you are not in the cloister because you are better than other people. On the contrary: those outside don't need all the support we have here in the monastery.

## Anselm Grün

There is a lovely story about a monk that says: don't imagine you are anything special; instead, imagine you are a dog that bites and so has to be kept on a leash.

*Brother David, I want to ask you what you think about the meaning of the contemplative life—and I don't mean the specific life of a monk. What are the most important steps to a fulfilled life? And how can I tell that I am advancing on the spiritual path?*

## David Steindl-Rast

From my experience I would answer: when everything is flowing well, and things are happening by themselves; when I don't have to do very much. I am not driven from without but from within. As to "flowing," you have to distinguish: It is one thing when a fish in the river uses the current to swim, and another when a bit of wood is simply carried along by the river. The fish makes use of the flow of the water and can even swim against the current, while the piece of wood simply moves passively. So: going with the flow of life is not being driven by the current but an active response to it.

In practice I find there are three steps: pause, become aware, respond. I have to build moments of stillness into my daily life, over and over again; otherwise the flow of my activity will drag me along with it. Pausing: that is the first point. Then comes the awareness: what opportunities is life offering me here and now? And in the third step I respond through my doing: I make use of the opportunity given. Those are three steps I return to again and again. Three steps—perhaps because I am from Vienna, and we dance our Viennese waltzes in three-quarter time. So: pause, become aware, and respond by doing. That seems to me to be the recipe for a fulfilled life.

## Anselm Grün

When you speak of pausing [*innehalten*]—after all, you are an expert in German language and literature, and the language here is marvelous. I have to hold *in* so that I can find a handle or a refuge within me, and then, when I have something to hold *to*, I can also turn outward.

*What, for you, are the signs that one is on a good spiritual path?*

### Anselm Grün

One part of it is internal peace, a radiating of goodwill and peace: that something blooms in the being of this person and she is capable of relationship. It was not for nothing that Benedict tested a monk to see if he really sought God. He saw this through three signs: whether he was zealous for worship, whether he was capable of entering into community, and whether he was prepared to allow himself to be challenged in work. In psychological terms those represent emotional ability, aptitude for community, and productive capacity. I think those are important aspects, and also, as you have said, not letting oneself be driven, being present to the moment, being able to surrender to the moment and the vis-à-vis.

There are people who long for quiet but cannot bear silence because they are afraid of their own stillness. Then you can see how driven they are. Being able to endure silence, placing oneself in the presence of silence and one's own truth that comes to the fore in it—that is contemplation. Contemplation is not staying stuck in yourself but getting through the chaos of thoughts and feelings to enter into the inner space of silence and there getting an intimation of being one with oneself and with God, the ground of all being. Out of that comes effective action. There are also people who are so fascinated by contemplation that they reject action. That is the danger of dropout mysticism. It is important that the quiet of contemplation flows into action. If I get hectic again, something is wrong.

We see that in the business world as well. There are companies that think they have to change constantly. They confuse leadership with stirring up the dust. They do a lot, but nothing comes of it. True transformation comes from quiet. Leaders who act out of calm have a broader perspective. When they change something, they do it well. In that sense we need the two poles to be effective in life. But we must not make contemplation a tool that lets us work better. It is only important that contemplation also express itself in how we shape our world. We see that, too, in the Our Father, the prayer at the heart of the Sermon on the Mount. The evangelist Matthew wants to tell us that the center is spiritual experience, but it has to work itself out in a different attitude. If I see the Sermon on the Mount—without prayer—as only a set of instructions for action, I get overwhelmed. I need prayer as well—contemplation as the center of action. Prayer alone—without any change of attitude—is only narcissism. Action without contemplation is only busyness. It is of the essence of the human that the two should come together.

**David Steindl-Rast**

I can see that you speak out of your rich experience as cellarer. I would summarize the center of Benedictine spirituality in one word: attention. That has become a fashionable word and is often misunderstood in a solipsistic way, so I will be more precise: it is about dialogical attention, total attention-in-relationship.

*Father Anselm pointed out earlier how important silence is if we are to become attentive, but that many people cannot exist in silence. What does silence show us? What comes to us when we listen to the silence?*

## David Steindl-Rast

If it is truly about silence, that is something one really should not talk about much. We can say something about it, but the essential can scarcely be put into words. Silence, after all, ultimately means that which is beyond all words.

## Anselm Grün

We distinguish between keeping silence and stillness. In the former case I have to do something: keep my mouth shut and bring my thoughts to silence as well. Stillness is something given. The space is still, the church is still, the forest is still, the mountain is still. Stillness comes from the verb "to place" and is related to "standing (still)."[54] It means taking account of what is. Stillness is a healing thing: the first step is keeping silence in the stillness, in self-encounter. The second step is letting go and becoming free. The third step is becoming one with myself, with the ground and the world around me, and ultimately becoming one with God. But many people are afraid of that, because in stillness everything that is within oneself comes to the fore. I might become aware that my life is somehow not right, or feelings of guilt arise, and then I always run away from myself.

## David Steindl-Rast

What you say reminds me of the three paths of mysticism: the *via purgativa*, the *via illuminativa*, and the *via unitiva*,[55] purification or inner clarification, enlightenment, and becoming one. It seems to me that self-encounter has a lot to do with clarification and that letting go is an interesting aspect of enlightenment. We no longer rely on our own little light but, instead, on what really is. In Psalm 36 we sing: "In your light we see light." At the end there lies the becoming-one with what is.

*If I understand that correctly, you have a different image of enlightenment from what we have learned from Buddhism?*

### Anselm Grün

What is called *satori*[56] in Buddhism is ultimately the third stage, the *via unitiva*. That is the goal of contemplation: that everything becomes clear, and I am one with all things. The *via illuminativa*, rather, is the way by which the divine light forces its way into us and drives out the darkness. In Christianity that is a continuation of the process of clarification.

### David Steindl-Rast

I want to point to a possible misunderstanding that could arise out of this way of speaking, because the false idea that God shines a light into the human being from without might be implied. I can tell that I myself am struggling for a better way of understanding it. Maybe we could say that the becoming-light and the becoming-one in the *via illuminativa* and *via unitiva* are a becoming-genuine—we discover our original aloneness on a higher level. If we say it that way there is less danger of being misunderstood in dualistic fashion.

### Anselm Grün

For Evagrius Ponticus,[57] becoming one with God is also becoming one with oneself and with everything that is. Peter Schellenbaum[58] says: "It is wonderful to be alone, all-one, one with everything." Becoming-one should not be seen primarily as becoming one with God. There is also an experience of unity in which I simply am and sense no one outside myself—only pure being. That is also a being-one, with the depth and the foundation. I think that is what St. Gregory[59] is describing when he says that Benedict saw the whole world in a single sunbeam. That is this shining through and being one with everything.

> *Can one say that in the contemplative life it is really about living out of solidarity, out of a bond with what sustains me and what also sustains you, that is, what addresses us in common in every moment?*

### Anselm Grün

Yes, I would say so. Contemplation means solidarity, and out of that solidarity saying "yes" to everything and everyone. Evagrius describes that inner bond as the sign of the contemplative monk: "A monk is someone who has separated himself from everything and yet feels bound to everything." Through this contemplative experience of solidarity our work acquires a different quality, when we realize that we are not alone but are directed toward one another. This doing together is important for the experience of community, for us Benedictines as well.

### David Steindl-Rast

The Latin word *contemplatio* contains the syllable *con-*, which indicates that it is always about two realities that have to be combined: God's will is to be realized "on earth as it is in heaven"—that is what contemplation is about. For the *templum*, which is also in the word "contemplation," was originally not an earthly temple but the measure and ordering of the heavens. *Con-templatio* was the projection of that eternal heavenly order into the transient earthly one. There is a saying in Hinduism: "If the measure of the temple is correct, the whole world is in the right order." The two belong together: looking to heaven and active organization of the world in light of what one sees there. Contemplation has to do justice to this twofold task. That is why the distinction between *actio* and *contemplatio* really rests on a misunderstanding. *Actio* is already contained within genuine *contemplatio*.

### Anselm Grün

Karlfried Graf Dürckheim[60] always advised meditating every morning and every evening. A student came to him and said: "I meditate every morning and every evening. I am on the way." Dürckheim answered him: "If your daily life is not practice, that is of no use at all." Another told him: "I am always in the presence of God." Dürckheim replied: "If you do not meditate every morning and every evening, that is of no use at all." We can see from this that there is a tension here. Normally we do need practice, but we must not become fixated on it. There are also people who have cultivated an inner contemplation and are no longer so fixated on external practices. And then there are those who meditate obsessively.

### David Steindl-Rast

There it is important to distinguish between meditation and contemplation. Through meditation we blend into the vision of the ideal image; through contemplation we make that ideal a reality. Meditation should serve contemplation. We should harmonize ourselves over and over again with the heavenly order through meditation and then try to make that order a reality in our chaotic lives.

Times for meditation are a part of contemplation. Let me clarify that with a simple example: Mother's Day. Here, Mother's Day represents meditation: one day in the year when we think about what our mother means to us and tell her so. But that doesn't mean that we only think of our mother once a year. We need that one Mother's Day so that we will honor her all the more on the other 364 days of the year. In the same way we need times of meditation so that, ultimately, our whole lives become contemplative.

*A lot of people today are not born into families that belong to a particular religious tradition, and they don't learn any religious tradition in the course of their education or in their professional life. There is a flood of offerings that claim to provide meaning, a host of healing traditions. The spirit of a lot of those offerings is not easy to see through. How can a seeker deal with the fact that she has no spiritual home anywhere and is simply overwhelmed by all the things that are offered? How can such a person find a reliable guide and an interpretation of the Mystery and the Holy that may encounter her in the thoroughly secular everyday world?*

## Anselm Grün

I would pay attention first of all to the language being used. When something is exorbitantly praised as the solution to all problems I am always skeptical. Every way involves practice. All the traditions that are rooted in ancient religious paths, such as Zen meditation in Buddhism or contemplative and ritual prayer in Christianity, are suitable. I am skeptical when entirely new strategies are invented for the purpose of solving problems. Those are never realistic.

## David Steindl-Rast

The real problem you are addressing is that we have no rituals. As far as the offerings are concerned, I would say: whatever helps is good. But it seems to me that the lives of future human beings are in danger through our loss of ritual and the fact that children grow up without these experiences of prayer. Like pollution of the environment and the oncoming change in the climate, the loss of ritual is dangerous for human life, for I believe that children need the experience of security and safety in their very being in order to lead an internally and externally steady life. We can scarcely convey such a thing to them except through authentic rituals[61] in which they can experience their embeddedness in strong relationships. If rituals do not help us to feel at home in the world while we are children, we lose all orientation.

## Anselm Grün

Disoriented and shapeless. Many children and young people today are restless and have psychic problems. We know that where living rituals are experienced there exists more security and sense of safety for them, and they are formed in a human way. Children and young people need a way of getting in contact with another reality: the transcendent, the divine. The handing on of faith has been interrupted in many families, or it does not succeed as it did before.

But I am sensing greater openness to ritual in our times. Sometimes—for example, when I am invited to a physicians' conference—I conclude my lecture with a stillness ritual so that the people have a sense of what happens if they simply listen to what is around them. Then I say a simple prayer in that stillness. Most people enjoy joining in. I can sense an openness.

But to get back to your question about the difference between real and false seminar offerings: it is not easy to determine whether something helps or not. Whenever I am manipulated, when I am urged to throw all my old thinking overboard, or when someone suggests that only with this particular program can I achieve a "higher level of consciousness," I get very skeptical. One's own freedom is important. Whatever it is, it dare not contradict my feelings. It must not drown me in what is totally foreign to me. What helps is only what corresponds to my own soul, and, therefore I pay attention to my feelings.

**David Steindl-Rast**

That is an important point. I have tried for years to find a clear distinction between helpful and harmful religious upbringing. As I see things today, the decisive difference lies in the goal that is aimed at—dependence and subordination, or independence.

If a community helps you to find your own freedom and stand on your own feet, it can be seen as positive. If it takes away your freedom and subjects you to fear, you have probably fallen prey to a sectarian cult.

The issue can be clearly seen in terms of Benedictine obedience. For a time you have to do what the abbot says. But the goal is that you learn to act freely, without anyone telling you what you ought to do. The goal of obedience is freedom. St. Benedict saw his monastery as a school for how to serve God—*schola Dominici servitii*. The danger in all schools—including in the monastery—is always that the students are not brought up to be independent but to be subordinated. A school should educate, not imprison.

*They are imprisoned because they remain manipulable and because the "tuition" is, of course, very lucrative for the guru or the leader.*

**Anselm Grün**

Clearly. You get the impression that in some spiritual traditions the masters need their students more than the other way around.

**David Steindl-Rast**

Yes, that is the great danger.

# Sin and Evil, or:

## *Why We Are Mired in Guilt*

*The biblical story of the Fall is not only one of the myths most frequently cited in the arts but also one of the most often misunderstood. A lot of people think it is about a first human couple, Adam and Eve, who—because they ate the fruit of the tree of knowledge— were driven out of Paradise by a jealous God and from then on had to suffer and die on earth. But the story makes no sense that way. Do we have to learn over again to understand that this is a myth, one that expresses eternal truth in the Bible but is repeated in the history of each individual?*

### Anselm Grün

The story of the Fall can be read in very different ways. In the first place, it is an image that tries to resolve the following problem: God created human beings as good, but the world is not only good; human beings are also evil. Thus this myth is an attempt to create an image to explain the origins of evil. Eugen Drewermann[62] wrote a long treatment in which he says that original sin is the fear of not being like God. The human being is dependent on God, but that is not what we want. The story of the Fall continues with Cain, who cannot bear it that his brother's sacrifice is preferred over his and therefore kills his brother. Then we get the account of the tower of Babel: people think they can

107

do everything as if they were God. The story of the Fall is meant to show us that people have not only positive but also negative tendencies that cause them to reject life's opportunities and fall short. In Greek, sin is called *hamartia*, which means "falling short of a goal" and rejecting one's own truth. The story of the Fall is not so much about Adam and Eve but about the mystery of evil. Ultimately, evil is as much a mystery as God is. It is not, however, an independent power alongside God, as if two gods were struggling for power, which is how some religions see it. Rather, there is only one God. The biblical image only tries to explain the origins of evil but ultimately it remains a mystery.

*Thomas Aquinas,*[63] *a Doctor of the Church, spoke of evil as a* privatio boni:[64] *evil is an "absence of good." Evil happens where the good that ought to be done is not done, where goodness is absent.*

### David Steindl-Rast

Evil is a vacancy where there ought to be something. I am most inclined to interpret the concept of "sin" in terms of the German word [*Sünde*], because then sin is connected with "*cutting* off" [ab*sondern*]. That makes it relatively easy to understand the concept and make it clear to others: whatever separates us from our Self, from others, and from the ground of our being—that is sin. If it does not do that, it is not sin, even if someone tries to tell you it is. It may violate social norms, but it is not sin. In saying that sin separates us from our Self, from others, and from the divine ground of being one may rearrange the order in any way, but the result remains the same. Whoever is separated from one of the three is also separated from the others. No one can say

"I get along wonderfully with myself but not with other people." There is something wrong with that. Separation is separation. But if you remain connected to your own innermost being, to your neighbor, and to God, you need have no fear. The same action (seen from without) can be sinful in one situation and not in another. The judgment of the action always depends on the situation. Of course, when we are weighing the question of sinfulness we always have to remember that we humans are masters of self-deception. Sin is separation. It is a lived "no" to belonging; hence it is unhealthy in every sphere.

*The concept of sin is also difficult in Christianity because we have different levels of meaning. For example, we talk about "original sin." Quite a few people have a naïve idea of that: In the beginning there was a human couple named Adam and Eve. They sinned and, as a result, the whole of humanity is in a mess. We can't do anything about our ancestors. But if we understand it that way the story makes little sense.*

### Anselm Grün

You don't have to believe in original sin. It is obvious that we exist in a world where a lot is out of joint. Original sin does not mean that we inherit something but just that this is how the world is. When we are born, we are born into a sick world. The Bible uses the image of the guilt of the ancestors but, of course, that is not meant biologically. It is not something that is inherited through conception.

**David Steindl-Rast**

Buddhists see it the same way. Every person who finds herself in the situation must experience it and name it this or that. "Original sin" is—we have to admit—a very unfortunate expression. Dissociation, break, separation, isolation are more accurate concepts. The notion of original sin[65] as commonly understood today was really invented by Augustine, and his own life story and personality certainly influenced him. The Buddhists name the same experience *dukkha*,[66] corresponding to Christian original sin. Behind *dukkha* was originally the idea of a wheel that is not correctly set on its axle, and so it drags. Everyone who looks at the world with open eyes realizes that this wheel cannot turn as it should. When Psalm 51:7 says "in sin my mother conceived me," that really means "my mother was part of a sinful world, a society out of joint, when I was conceived."

*Alas, that is usually heard in a completely different way, namely, as if the sexual act of procreation were something sinful for which one ought to feel guilty.*

**David Steindl-Rast**

We have to admit that it is heard differently because—out of a misunderstanding of the idea—it has been preached differently.

## Anselm Grün

The topic of sexuality and sin has been one of the church's worst shadow sides. That is also connected with celibacy, because priests who had renounced sexuality were fixated on it and constantly overemphasized it. We simply have to see that for what it was. We have to free ourselves from a fixation on sin and sexuality. In the Middle Ages it was not as extreme as it was in the nineteenth century and up to the 1950s.

## David Steindl-Rast

That had more to do with a Victorian prudery that was very widespread in the church, and unfortunately it is still having negative effects. But that brings us to a very different topic: tradition, which has to be constantly refreshed. Every tradition must repeatedly return to its sources and renew itself. That is an area in which we ought to welcome and affirm a great deal that comes to us from secular culture: a positive evaluation of the body, of the feminine, of the sexual. Those are values that belong from the beginning to what is Christian, but that we have lost.

*But back to sin. Is sin something that a human being as such, that is, because he is a human being, cannot avoid?*

## Anselm Grün

C. G. Jung says that it would be naïve to think that a human being can avoid sin. There is no life in which we are not more or less guilty. Certainly there is a human tendency to think that we can always keep our hands clean, but Jung says that we always fall a little short. Jesus told the parable of the unjust manager (Luke 16:1-13) about that. Whether we want to or not, we always waste a little of our wealth. The question is: How do we deal with our guilt? Jesus took a very sober attitude toward it. His parable about the unjust manager answers the question of how I can deal with my guilt without losing my self-respect. There are two possibilities: either work hard and make an effort, or feel guilty, kneel down, and beg. Jesus says no to both options. He shows us a different way. We should say, with the manager: "I am guilty, and you are guilty. So let's share our guilt. I will go honestly into your house, and you may come honestly into mine." Guilt opens me to other people. I get down off the throne of my own self-righteousness and become a human being among others. That is Jesus' message.

Imposing feelings of guilt is a subtle form of the exercise of power. And of course the church has made use of it, and it happens even today when parents cause their children to have a bad conscience and exercise power in that way.

*In the third chapter of Romans we read: "Jesus Christ died for our sins," and in the* Exsultet, *the Easter hymn, we even sing, "O* felix culpa—*O happy fault, that merited a Redeemer so holy and so great." How do you understand that?*

## Anselm Grün

"Died for our sins" means concretely: the sin was Pilate's cowardice, the intrigues of the high priests, the betrayal by Judas—sin was the cause of Jesus' death. But we must not fixate on redemption in terms of sin. One thing is true above all: God forgives because God is God and not because Jesus died. The death of Jesus does not cause forgiveness. We have to see that correctly in terms of dogma. Karl Rahner says: Jesus' death on the cross mediates the forgiveness of sins. It is on the cross that God's forgiving love is most visible.

This theology is given to us by the one Greek among the evangelists: Luke. He has no concept of sacrifice and atonement. When Jesus himself forgives his murderers from the cross we can trust all the more that there is nothing in us that God cannot forgive. People have a longing for forgiveness and at the same time an internal resistance to it, according to the model: If I am really guilty, I don't believe in God's forgiveness. Here the cross is helpful in making us believe in God's forgiving love, but we should not imagine that Jesus had to die in order for God to forgive. That is nonsense. Likewise, to believe that God sulks in a corner and then comes out and forgives us is absurd. That would be a trivial image of God. God gives us the unconditional love of Jesus on the cross in order that we may be able to believe in his forgiving love.

## David Steindl-Rast

I would underline that several times. Jesus' message is that God has forgiven us; we might say even before we have sinned. There is no before and after with God. Sin is already forgiven from before time.

### Anselm Grün

Paul Tillich[67] calls forgiveness the acceptance of the unacceptable. Anyone who is guilty feels himself unacceptable. What helps him to be able to accept himself again? He needs people who accept him, and the experience that God accepts him. That experience can happen in words, but Tillich points out that the image of the cross has helped very many to believe in forgiveness.

### David Steindl-Rast

But here we have to emphasize that what we are trying to express is the original, central Christian message. You and I agree in this conviction, but whole libraries have been written to contradict what we are saying here.

### Anselm Grün

I wrestled intensely with the question of redemption even during my theology studies, first starting from Karl Rahner, and then through Paul Tillich as well. If we look in the Bible, we see that both the apostles Luke and John get by without using the idea of redemption. For John, the cross means that Jesus loved us to the end. From the cross he will draw all things to himself. The cross means that I am embraced, with all my contradictions, my wounds, and my guilt. There are two passages in Paul where he speaks of redemption. The German "unified translation," however, has it backward. Christ has become redemption for us: here the image is that of the redemptive cover—the cover of the Ark of the Covenant—but that is just an image. It does not say that Jesus achieved redemption; that is nowhere in the Bible. Unfortunately, that is how the unified translation has it.[68] Romans 3:25 means that Jesus has become the place of redemption. In his love he has become a sponge that draws all sin into itself and cleanses it.

We can also look at another biblical passage: "Behold the Lamb of God, who takes away the sin of the world."[69] Some exegetes immediately see that as a reference to atonement, but it has nothing to do with that. Rather, it means: Jesus has become flesh—the Greek *sarx* means "what is mortal." And the word for lamb here is not *arnion*, the lamb sacrificed for atonement, but *amnōs*, which means the "vulnerable," "pure," "sinless." And the words "takes away the sin of the world" come originally from the book of Exodus, where God tells Moses: I am a merciful God. I do not lay sin upon you. I take away sin. In Jesus the love of God that takes away sin is revealed. Flesh (*sarx*), lamb (*amnōs*), and cross (*stauros*)—those are the summit of vulnerability. And that the cross is the lifting up, the perfection—that is the paradox.

## David Steindl-Rast

Understanding Jesus' death as atonement is only one of many interpretations in the New Testament, but this one was selected and theologically developed almost to the exclusion of the others. We have a lot of neglected opportunities to catch up with. If we want to understand more accurately what redemption is about, it seems to me that a statement in John's gospel is important; there Jesus says, "I came that they may have life, and have it abundantly" (John 10:10). This abundant life is liberation from our narrowness and our little ego. It is a liberation *from* encapsulation in sin and *into* community, not only with other people but also with the animals, the plants, and the whole universe. It is about reunion, becoming once again a part of the whole and, with that whole, praising God through joyful, grateful living. For me that is redemption, and not that sin is a dirty spot on my vest that has to be washed away by redemption.

### Anselm Grün

Redemption, *sōteria*, also means healing, well-being, and rescue. The Greek verb *sōzein* also means protecting and becoming whole. The human being experiences herself as damaged, wounded, and separated. She wants to be whole. She needs a space in which to become whole and not remain fragmented. For me the cross is a symbol before which I sit and meditate, again and again. The cross was already a symbol of salvation, even before Jesus, symbolizing the unity of all objects. The early church saw the cross as a tree of life, a ladder, and a key to life. It is a mystery that Jesus died on the cross, but we must not link that with images of punishment and atonement; instead, we must associate it with love to the very end. After all, Jesus also says, "No one has greater love than this, to lay down one's life for one's friends" (John 15:13).

On the Mount of Olives, Jesus faced the great question whether he should give up or follow his path to the end. This love to the end was his motive. But Jesus did not come in order to die; he came to preach his message of the reign of God. In the end, the political situation conflicted with his intent.

When we celebrate the death and resurrection of Jesus in the Eucharist, for me that is a wisdom, an art of transforming whatever happens to me into an act of surrender. For me, sacrifice means surrender. I have sacrificed my life—in the Greek translation of the Bible it says "gambled it." That shows us the value Jesus sets on us. We are worth so much to him that he gambled his life for our sake. We also find this paradox in the Gospel of John. Jesus' death is violent; it comes from without. But Jesus transforms that violence into an act of love. In doing so he seizes power from evil and violence and transforms it. That is the paradox. There are many images like that, and we can never finish with meditating on this mystery. But we must not freeze it into meaning atonement and guilt.

# The Doctrine of Seven Deadly Sins, or:

## The Beginnings of a Spiritual Psychology

*The biblical texts, as well as the spiritual writings of the Desert Mothers and Fathers, developed a wise religious psychology for dealing with temptations. Evagrius Ponticus, one of the great Desert Fathers of the fourth century, produced something like a first psychology of the spiritual life, the teaching about the so-called nine* logismoi.[70] *Later, as the "eight vices," it was handed on by John Cassian[71] and others and became more widely known as the doctrine of the seven deadly sins. In the original doctrine of vices Evagrius shows how monks should deal with the passions. At that time people used the image of demons with which one had to fight, but this was not a demonology, as if it were about spirits lurking outside. Rather, these are images of the drives within us. What should people today know about this doctrine of eight vices in order to make better progress in the spiritual life?*

### Anselm Grün

Viewed for the moment in value-free terms, the *logismoi* are passions. Passions are forces that control people but can also drive them into life. It is not a matter of suppressing or excising my passions, for then I would be weak and my spirituality would lack strength. It is about getting free from being pathologically yoked to the passions. The Greek word *apatheia*[72] does not mean we should no longer have passions, but instead describes a condition in which the passions are integrated and we are no longer controlled by them. Let's look, for example, at the basic drives for food, sexuality, and possession.

The word "drive" already tells us that something is pushing at us. We want to eat because we want to enjoy it. We want sexuality because we have a longing to surrender and forget ourselves. Behind possessions lies the longing for rest. All three drives have likewise been religiously elevated: the sacred meal, sexuality in mysticism and divine ecstasy, and as for possessions, Jesus speaks of the treasure in the field, the costly pearl. Yet all three can likewise become addictions: eating, sex, having things. There is something positive in the passions and drives, but they can also rule over us. It is always about the right balance. The Desert Father Poimēn[73] says: "When the passions come and you engage in give-and-take with them, they will make you more tried and tested."[74] So I must not cut myself off from them but struggle with them in order to integrate their positive features into my life.

The emotional passions are sadness, anger, and sluggishness. Sorrow, Greek *pentos*, is part of being human. Psychology says this too: I have to be sad that I am as average as I am, and when I have regretted it, I can accept myself as I am. But sadness—*lypē*—as a vice means remaining stuck in sadness, in self-pity. At the base of this self-pity lie exaggerated, infantile desires. In self-pity I focus on myself and don't get on with life. Anger—Greek *orgē*—also has its positive side. Aggression is meant to regulate the relationship between intimacy and distance. But anger can also govern me in the form of violent temper or when I "flip out." Sluggishness, or melancholy—*akēdia*—is basically the inability to live in the moment. I don't want to work or pray or enjoy or do anything. I am inwardly torn, and it's always other people's fault.

## David Steindl-Rast

Because I have a tendency to fits of temper myself, I have always liked the fact that Thomas Aquinas took a generally positive attitude toward anger—as an extra portion of energy that we need in order to overcome resistance, just as when we are driving a car we give it more gas when we're going up a steep hill. The negative aspect of anger is really only impatience.

## Anselm Grün

That would be aggression in a positive sense. There are still the three spiritual passions: envy, ambition, and pride; the last of the three—*hybris*—is the most dangerous. There is something quite positive behind ambition if one wants to achieve something. The negative side appears when someone wants to be constantly admired and applauded. Then she makes herself totally dependent on external recognition. Envy occurs when we constantly compare ourselves with others. We look at the others and think they always have it better. That is also a way in which I am not present to myself.

And *hybris*, pride, is the refusal to accept myself as I am. Instead, I cling to an exalted ideal image and refuse to look at my reality. C. G. Jung speaks of *hybris* as an "inflation of the ego." I puff myself up with great images. Jung talks of the danger of identifying with archetypal images. One example would be the image of the healer and helper. Archetypal images serve a positive function by coaxing more vitality out of me. Each of us is a healer and helper in some field. The image awakens our energy. But if we identify with it we become blind to the fact that we are living out our own needs under the cloak of being a helper and healer.

For example, a woman told me that when she was seventeen she had been raped by her brother. She went to confession, and her confessor told her: "I can heal you." That was quite a promise! The "healing" consisted in the woman having to go to confession every four weeks, where the priest held her in his arms for an hour at a time. She found it odd, but she thought the priest must know what he was doing. She was forty years old before she was able to say: "What a pig! He filled his own need to be close to me under the cloak of being my healer."

That kind of thing is dangerous. There is a fundamental danger in spirituality that I may identify totally with the Holy. The Holy is in us, but if I identify completely with it I become blind to the fact that I am answering other needs under that spiritual cloak.

### David Steindl-Rast

Excessive ambition builds a pompous palace with higher and higher stories: *hybris* lives on the top floor and has all the lower floors torn out.

In our monastery in Mount Savior the teaching of early monasticism about vices and virtues is presented in this way: our goal is to be awake in the Now. We can fall short of the goal in three ways: we can neglect the Now because we cling to the past or are already dreaming of the future. If neither of those is the case, there is a third way of avoiding the Now: we can sleep it away. All the other vices spring from those three roots. So, for example, when we hold grudges, exhibit envy, pettiness, or penny-pinching, or engage in excessive eating, drinking, sex, and luxury, we are not open to the unique new opportunity the Now offers us, because we cling to what we already know from the past. Contrariwise, we can miss the Now through angry impatience, jealousy and resentment, love of money, desire for fame, and similar involvements in wishful dreams for our future. But even without clinging to the future or the past we can avoid the Now, for example, through indolence, melancholy, tepidity, tedium, or that lack of interest at every level that was called *akēdia* and is said to come from the midday devil of the desert heat. This view simplifies the catalogue of vices to three and at the same time makes it understandable why they damage us: they hamstring our alert response to the opportunity the Now gives us.

But by means of this simple scheme we can also see that each of these potentially negative inclinations has something positive about it. In a community it is not hard to see who is inclined to get stuck, who is always ahead of the others, and who feels at home in the moderate middle. But each of those three groups has something important to contribute to the life of the whole. The "conservatives" and the "progressives" correct one another. And if it gets too hot between the two groups we need the third kind of brothers, because they look for balance so that the boat doesn't tip. They keep everything stable with the ballast of their *gravitas*.

Each of us, by nature, is inclined to one of those three attitudes. Each of us has his light and shadow sides. What we have to do is recognize and develop the light side of our natural inclination. Vices are bad habits that have become second nature to us, but we can also make good habits our second nature, our virtues. Two steps are necessary. If, in the first step, we recognize our inclination, in the second step we can ask what our likely virtues are, virtues that come easy to us because our natural inclination already pushes us passionately in that direction.

*How do we deal with these passions in a good way?*

### Anselm Grün

Sorrow invites me to accept myself in my average condition, to accept that I cannot fulfill all my wishes. Anger, as a strength, invites me to undertake something and change some state of things. The *akēdia* that tears me apart is healed by *stabilitas*, as I learn to be with myself. Love of fame can spur me to be active. Evagrius says: the monk who loves fame should fast, live ascetically, and so struggle against the primitive passions. The positive impulse of envy is that I will not be content but sense by comparison that I have other possibilities. Only I dare not stay stuck in envy, because it will turn me green. Envy is an invitation to view my opportunities with gratitude. *Hybris* has a positive side if I allow myself to be inspired by ideals and so evoke my abilities. The danger is that I will identify with those ideals and so suppress my reality.

*That is what Wolfgang Schmidbauer[75] described in his book about the destructiveness of ideals. I replace the real with the ideal. I no longer believe in myself; instead, I make my ideal "I" the center of all things. In such a refusal of self-acceptance one exists, so to speak, in the soul's hell.*

### Anselm Grün

That is why humility, *humilitas*, is so important if I am to keep both feet on the ground. Among priests, for example, I find again and again that they identify very much with their role but have no solid basis. Let me tell you about one circumstance: there are priests who can no longer celebrate because they are afraid of getting dizzy at the altar. That is a sign that my ideal image of myself is too big, and I see that I am really quite different. When the distance between the ideal and the reality gets too wide, it can make one dizzy. Ideals can elicit things from us. When we read the lives of the saints, a lot of that can be stimulating, but danger arises when we think we have to copy them exactly.

### David Steindl-Rast

Fundamentally, the answer to the question of how we are to deal with our weaknesses and vices is that we should not fight them but find the positive element in them and then develop the positive that is closest to who I am.

### Anselm Grün

I would just quote the beginning of the tale of the three languages. The young son of a count learns the language of barking dogs. The enraged father expels his son. The son arrives at a castle where he wants to spend the night. The lord of the castle can only offer him the tower where the barking dogs are kept; they have already bitten some people. But the boy who understands the dogs' language gets along with them. They tell him that they are only vicious because they are guarding a treasure. They show it to him and help him dig it up.

For me that is a helpful image to use in spiritual direction. Where someone has the greatest problems—this one with sexuality, another with bad temper, still another with excessive sensitivity—that is where his treasure is buried. The loudest dog is the one that points to the treasure.

*The desert monks, and later a good many mystics and spiritual teachers, point out how important it is to be watchful and wise in distinguishing good from evil. But as everyone knows, that is not an easy job, because much that appears to be good, if we look carefully, turns out to be hidden evil. And much that appears to be evil turns out, in fact, to be good. That means that in one's life one needs a clear head to untangle all that—what the tradition calls "discernment of spirits." What criteria for discernment would you recommend for discovering the truth?*

### Anselm Grün

The monks have four criteria: that is always good where greater vitality, freedom, peace, and love exist. The ancient monks distinguished three kinds of thoughts: those that come from God, those that come from demons, and those that come out of myself. The thoughts that come from God effect vitality, freedom, peace, and love. The thoughts from demons cause excessive demands, narrowness, and anxiety. And the thoughts that come from me are characterized by vagueness, banality, and distraction.

*I want to interrupt here briefly because you spoke of demons. I think it would be intellectually foolhardy to picture demons as spirits lurking somewhere outside. I think we have to understand them in terms of depth psychology. Today we would speak of spiritual and systemic entanglements. Idiomatically—at least in Austria—we have a very nice way of describing what is "demonic": it's got him.[76] He is entangled in some craziness or addiction. Is that what demons are?*

### Anselm Grün

Here again theology is important. It says that demons as well as angels are created spiritual beings and personal powers, but they are not persons one can distinguish individually. There are powers that damage my person. That has a social dimension through social entanglements and wounds in childhood and so on. When we speak of demons, we mean the depth dimensions of evil.

C. G. Jung once asked: "Which is more realistic? To say 'I am being ridden by the devil,' or 'I have a complex'?" He thought it was more appropriate psychologically to say one is being ridden by the devil. He didn't see the devil as a person; he meant it as an image. As you say, "It's got me," something is riding me. When I say, "I have a complex," I think that *I* have the complex. But in reality, the complex has me.

That is the image of the demonic, but we always have to be clear that it is an image. I know some Christians who talk too much about demons and possession. They project something outward that is really inside them. When someone constantly speaks of the devil, she really is in fear of her own soul.

### David Steindl-Rast

I agree with what you said about discernment of spirits, but there is another approach that interests me. Discernment of spirits can be understood in two ways: either distinguishing good spirits from bad spirits with more and more clarity or distinguishing between those who think they can clearly discern which spirits are which and those who accept the world quite realistically, as it is, and in that case it is not so easy to make a clear distinction. I have always wished that there were a St. George who would be clearly recognizable from his halo, and who kills the dragon—*he*, of course, is easily recognized because of the smell of his breath! But wherever I look, in reality, the dragon also wears a little halo, and St. George has a dragon's tail. So: I find clear distinctions only in books—and nowhere in real life.

### Anselm Grün

Yes, they are always mixed up. How often it happens that something bad is going on, but it is screened by the good. Jesus always flayed self-righteousness. It is not always absolutely clear what is good and what is bad. There is no chemical separator. The mixture is always there.

# Suffering and Reconciliation, or:

## The Cross and the Structures of Sin

Sometimes, in our striving for a "good life," we try not to think about suffering. We normally avoid suffering when we can. That is understandable. But, interestingly, the Gospel teaches that life is also an experience of the cross. That does not mean that we ought to seek out suffering, certainly not that we should sacralize it. But it seems to be the case that suffering is unavoidable in life, even on the spiritual path. If that is so: what is the deeper meaning of suffering?

### Anselm Grün

I know of two attitudes. One is anxiety. A young woman came to me; she was very pretty, successful. Everything had gone well in her life so far. She came because she was afraid it couldn't go on. Soon there would have to be suffering. But that is the wrong way to look at things. Suffering need not come. But for the most part it does. We have no guarantee of getting through life without suffering, but we should not be masochists and go looking for it. Experience shows that suffering encounters us: through an illness, a conflict, or a hard loss. Then it is important to accept the challenge. I cannot explain why there is suffering, but I can influence how I meet it. For me, the Christian answer is: suffering shatters my ideas of myself, my life, and God. But when my ideas are broken, I am not; instead, I will be broken out to my true Self, others, and God. If I cling to another idea, such as "I have led a good life; why did God let me fall ill?" I will become bitter and be broken by it.

### David Steindl-Rast

In this context we have to be careful how we use the word "cross." The original cross was the thwarting of Jesus' plans. We should put more emphasis on the fact that Jesus was not executed by lawful judicial means. The Romans used crucifixion as the legal punishment for high treason and for runaway slaves: their crime was that they undermined the established social order. But what was the aim of Jesus' preaching of the reign of God if it was not to undermine the ruling order of society? Consequently, he could foresee that his way must lead to the cross, and that is why the biblical passages in which Jesus predicts his crucifixion make perfect historical sense. Anyone who pushes against the power pyramids of the world in that way and preaches completely different values will fall beneath the wheels and be executed. That was the real reason for Jesus' crucifixion. Anyone could have predicted it. When we follow Jesus it means that we take up our own crosses, because following Jesus quite explicitly means undermining the ruling order of society, even today. That is something radically revolutionary.

### Anselm Grün

The cross is not just something passive. Jesus had the courage to think differently and to follow his conscience. Martin Luther King Jr. and others have done the same. They did not seek the cross, but they fought for justice. The cross was the result. They had to reckon with it. People in Latin America who act for justice must also expect to be pursued by some kind of death squads or mercenaries.

### David Steindl-Rast

We have to say that clearly. When we, as Christians, are challenged to take up the cross it means that we are challenged to overturn the existing unjust orders of society—but not by violence. We need a revolution that is so revolutionary that it even revolutionizes the idea of revolution. Otherwise, only those who previously were on the bottom will sit on top and do the same as those before them. But the whole unjust pyramid of power has to be torn down and replaced by a web of small networks, small communities. Those who were responsible for the first such communities in Jerusalem simply said to officialdom: "We must obey God rather than any human authority" (Acts 5:29). The reign of God begins with tangible small communities that act without fear because they have freed themselves from a logic of power that produces injustice. Therefore, in my opinion, monasticism is fundamentally revolutionary.

*Where today do you see the conditions we could call "structures of sin?"[77] What situations necessarily call for a revolution in the sense you have described?*

### David Steindl-Rast

The "structures of sin" are revealed in the pyramids of power that characterize our civilization. It bears all the signs of ego—above all, fear. The three principal characteristics of the power pyramid are then rooted in fear: violence, competitive struggle, and greed. Jesus, in contrast, fearlessly presents the reign of God: freedom from violence, cooperation, and sharing. Against our insane nuclear armaments stands nonviolence: "all who take the sword will perish by the sword" (Matt 26:52). Against the dishonest competition that has become the engine driving our whole culture stands cooperation for the common good: "bear one another's burdens" (Gal 6:2). And against greed, avarice, and enrichment at the expense of others, by which the wealthy get richer and richer and the poor get poorer and poorer, Jesus sets sharing: "whoever has two coats must share with anyone who has none" (Luke 3:11). The story of the multiplication of the loaves[78] shows us that when there is sharing there is always enough for everyone. In these three areas—armaments, competitive struggle, and greed—Christianity must be revolutionary.

### Anselm Grün

Three points: The pure economization of the whole of life is a danger today because everything is regarded from a purely economic standpoint. This is true in medicine, in education, in Nature, and so on. Second, regulation of everything through laws is problematic. Law and justice are drifting farther and farther apart. Sometimes the law is even misused in complicated situations to fix on one guilty party and make it all about him. The third critical point is injustice in all its dimensions. Jesus calls happy the people who hunger and thirst for justice (Matt 5:6). Whoever sows justice will reap peace. There is always injustice in the sense that there is no absolute justice. But Christians must always advocate for just structures, just distribution of goods, and just distribution of opportunities. Today we live in the age of globalization. That could be an opportunity for more justice. But if only the power of the strongest conquers, globalization will be a curse for humanity. It will be important to globalize our Christian values as a counterweight to power and violence.

### David Steindl-Rast

At the roots of this fundamental evil you have named lie fear and greed. In fact, greed springs from fear of not having enough, of falling short. And there we are back to the ego. We live in a world built by ego. Our world bears all the characteristic signs of the ego. But we have to find our way to a world of the "I-Self."

*I want to follow up on one of the suggestions you mentioned in connection with the revolutionary inheritance. We can easily illustrate it by the example of suffering, because suffering is omnipresent in the world. There is suffering caused by misfortune, illness, or natural catastrophes, and that kind is unavoidable. But there is a great deal of suffering that is humanly caused and could have been avoided. History, spirituality, and even psychology show us, one way or another, that those who do not learn to transform the pain of suffering will usually turn it against others. We see again and again how the cycle of violence and counterviolence, act and retribution, injustice and hatred repeats itself. This kind of suffering is also a "bedrock of atheism"[79] because atheism sees a good God as irreconcilable with a world that suffers. What does Christian tradition teach about the transformation of pain and the meaning of suffering?*

## Anselm Grün

To begin with: every one of us is wounded, like it or not. If we do not come to terms with these wounds, it often happens that we pass them along. Then that cycle of suffering happens. For me, the cross is a stop sign. Jesus is wounded, but he transforms that woundedness into an act of love.

*A brief follow-up: That sounds very heroic. I have to reconcile myself with a wound. Consider, if you will, the victims of abuse. It is not so easy for them to be reconciled. I have to first accept and be able to say that I have been abused. And I have to be allowed to be angry about it.*

## Anselm Grün

Yes, you are speaking of the process of forgiveness. It has five steps:

First: The pain must not be passed over or repressed; it has to be allowed to exist. Taking myself seriously also means taking my pain seriously.

Second: I have to allow my rage to exist. Rage is the power to distance myself from others and so to free myself from others' power over my life. But rage has to be transformed into ambition: I myself can live. I am not simply a victim of abuse.

Third: I must objectively understand what has really happened. Only when I can understand it can I assert myself.

The fourth step is forgiving. Forgiveness is an act of liberation. It means that I free myself from the negative energy that is in me because of my wound. I also free myself from my ties to the others, because if I cannot forgive, I remain bound, and the other still has power over me.

The fifth step would be to transform the wound into a "pearl." I have been wounded, but as a result I have started out and been sent on a new path. I know deeply wounded people who have succeeded in transforming their woundedness into a "pearl." As a result they have become good therapists, physicians, or pastors of souls and can help other wounded people. That is the transformation of the wound into a pearl.

Of course, we must not judge, for I know people whose stories take my breath away when I hear them. I know that in such cases a transformation will not be possible in a short time. Then I sometimes say: You have experienced something horrible. But you have been through it, and that in itself makes you more experienced than other people. You can be proud that you survived it. The question is now: How can you live with it?

### David Steindl-Rast

I want to say something more about forgiveness. The word "forgiveness" itself speaks to me because it is the most intensive form of giving. In Latin, too, there is the word *perdonare*, which means giving entirely, the utmost giving.

The prior stage is giving up. We always have to give up something in life; otherwise nothing new can come. We have to give up childhood to become adults. In the end we have to give up our whole life. But the gesture of giving up is also one of lifting up, because when we give something up we do not let it fall. Mothers have to give up their children so that they can mature, but they do not let them fall.

The next stage is surrender, which is much harder than giving up. That to which we surrender ourselves breaks our hearts. When we take something into our hearts, our hearts break open. With these open hearts, we can forgive.

*Shouldn't we distinguish between forgiveness and reconciliation? Psychologically, it seems to me, we have to do that, because it can happen that I am injured by people who can no longer be reached or who are already dead. Then I can no longer deal with the other party about the guilt. But I can forgive, even though I cannot be reconciled with the other. Likewise, when there is too strong an involvement with the other person as a result of violent acts it may be that reconciliation is not possible, but through forgiveness I can at least free myself and live in a new relationship.*

### Anselm Grün

I have not understood forgiveness so much in terms of the Latin *perdonare* as in the sense of *dimittere*, giving or sending something away or leaving it with another. Both are surely important. Giving away means that the other is still my opponent, but I leave what has happened with her and so do not permit her any more power. Certainly *perdonare*, in the sense of feeling one with oneself, as you have suggested, is more intense. But sometimes it is enough simply to leave it with the other.

### David Steindl-Rast

Then it is not so in-depth . . .

## Anselm Grün

That is true. In that case I am first of all present to myself, and I am freed. Reconciliation [German *Versöhnung*] has to do with the verb *sühnen* [to atone or avenge]. In Latin, from which the English word comes, it is *reconciliatio*—restoring community. You referred to that previously: that we are together. The one point is that I am reconciled with myself and with the other. But often the other remains unreconciled. I experience that often among siblings when the issue is a common inheritance. They want to be reconciled, but the inheritance tears everything apart. The question then is: Can I be internally reconciled independent of the other? I am open, but I am also helpless if the other remains unreconciled. Then there is no point in opening myself totally.

## David Steindl-Rast

We might also say that in order to bring about reconciliation there must be at least two who forgive one another. But if one does not forgive, the other can still do so. One can forgive independently of the other, but reconciliation can only happen when both are ready for it.

## Anselm Grün

But I can at least be reconciled with myself.

# Spiritual Growth, or:

## *Learning to Accept Myself as I Really Am*

*Some people imagine that a religious person is perfect, and a holy life is "perfect," "pure," "clean," and "harmonic." But people are not like that. Their lives are always a mixture of many different ambitions and experiences. There are holy things in this life, but there are also abysmal ones. Life is complex and often paradoxical. We also have to learn to live through trial and error. So, how do we grow spiritually—by always doing things "right" or by doing them "wrong"?*

### Anselm Grün

Of course we should try to act "rightly," but even though we attempt it, we do some things "wrongly." Learning by trial and error is one thing. The other is: whoever encounters himself also encounters his shadow side. Through that he becomes aware of his fragility and abysses. When I was in the novitiate I really did not like humility because I thought of it as something negative. The older I have become, the more I sense that humility is the appropriate attitude by which to accept oneself with one's strengths and weaknesses. Then, in spite of everything, I can feel myself accepted by God and don't have to judge everyone else. Jesus' demand that we not judge is not so much a moral maxim; behind it lies the experience that one who knows oneself no longer desires to judge others.

**David Steindl-Rast**

On the one hand, we have to say: accept yourself as you are. But the ideal of being better has the advantage that we try harder because we want to achieve it. Lacking it, we may become very negligent, and that, too, is a danger.

**Anselm Grün**

That is why it is a basic principle that I can only change what I have accepted. The first step is acceptance. But I want to grow and not just stand still; otherwise I'll get lazy. Standing still is one danger, and that is why, for example, we read the Bible and the lives of the saints in order to sense that there is more potential in us. The other danger is projection. Some people consider the two of us holy. They project something onto us and then are disappointed that we are just human too. On the other hand, some people need such projection screens, but we must never identify with them.

**David Steindl-Rast**

There is an important book on the growth process you refer to, by James Fowler, titled *Stages of Faith*.[80] As Jean Piaget[81] tried to describe the development of intelligence, so Fowler sketched religious development. He was able to show that the crucial step in the transition from one plateau of development to the next always emerges from a crisis. That is a valuable insight because it teaches us how important the crises of life are. What you call transformation is the result of a crisis. A *krisis*, in the sense of the Greek word, winnows out what is able to survive and what is not.

*Does that mean that the Christian spirit also includes what is imperfect?*

### Anselm Grün

Obviously. The Christian spirit is acceptance: that we are accepted unconditionally. But it also has a goal, and that goal is that we become more and more permeable to Christ and our true Self. We never get to the end of that. This process of purification and transformation causes what is proper to us to emerge more and more strongly and what does not belong to our lives to shrink. It continues to our death. But it is never the case that we thereby become perfect people. For me it is very important that the spirit of Christ also shines through our weaknesses. We only want to radiate Christ through our strengths, but we do so through our wounds too.

### David Steindl-Rast

Leonard Cohen has written a beautiful song called "Anthem," that says:

> Ring the bells that still can ring,
> forget your perfect offering.

> There is a crack in everything,
> that's how the light gets in. [82]

He is pointing out that it is better to celebrate the positive than to try to rub out the negative. The song marvelously expresses a deep spiritual insight. No one could say it better.

## Anselm Grün

Henri Nouwen always said: where we are broken, the masks we have donned and the armor around our hearts are also broken. We are broken open to our true Self, and then something can shine through.

# Roots and Growth, or:

## *Linking Old and New*

*In the Christian churches we see a considerable tension, a great gulf between the so-called conservatives and the so-called progressive-liberals. The conservatives can be roughly sketched as those who want to do the old in the old spirit. The liberal wants to do the new—but also in the old spirit. Both have struggled throughout history as antagonists, but there seems to be no escape because both are based on dualistic thinking. Can there be a third way? Something we might call a contemplative-integrative view beyond these two poles?*

### Anselm Grün

For me what is crucial is whether you have a heart. Abba Pambo, an early desert monk, says: "If you have a heart, you can be saved." There are conservatives who have a heart. In my heart I am also conservative because tradition is important to me. But the conservative heart must also be broad and open. The tradition must always be filled with a new spirit and translated into our own time. Liberals, on the other hand, pose important questions in new ways. But when it gets to be a matter of who is right, then it gets difficult.

The tension between preservation and the new lies in every one of us. We have to resolve that tension if we want to stay alive. If we throw away the old and only pursue the new, our roots die. But if we cling tenaciously to the old, it can't grow and develop. So we have to recognize this tension within each of us in our common life as well.

*But how can Christianity free itself from dualistic thinking?*

### Anselm Grün

Dualism is always a struggle over who is right. I have counseled some stubborn, hardened people. Most of them were driven by anxiety. A priest once said to me: "I am afraid of getting bogged down; that is why I need such rigorist forms." It was important for him that he gradually strengthen his Self so he would no longer need that kind of narrowness. But no one can take away the narrowness from outside, because then he would really bog down. For the moment one has to leave it as it is and consider how it can be opened and broadened.

### David Steindl-Rast

What you say about the heart is the crucial element. The answer to the question is already there. Some do the old thing with an old spirit. Others do the new thing with an old spirit. Both need to do the old and the new with a new spirit. After all, Psalm 51 implores: "Create in me a new heart."

The old is usually regarded as stiff and stodgy and the young as flexible and fluid. In that sense we all need a renewed heart and a new spirit. No matter whether our preference is for the old or the new, or something in between—it all depends on the heart. The heart represents connection. We are all bound together in our hearts.

In our Christian tradition there are always two great misunderstandings that create a danger for a genuine heartfulness: one is that our relationship to God is interpreted juridically. Sin, judgment, commandment, retribution, and reconciliation thus acquire an importance that does not belong to them.

The second misunderstanding lies in interpreting our relationship to God in a private sense: only God and *I* instead of God and *we*. But Jesus' utmost concern was the reign of God. He was about building community. In the reign of God, community with God presupposes community with other people—heart to heart.

# The Incarnation, or:

## How Body, Soul, and Spirit Go Together

*A tradition that has profoundly shaped our thinking in the Christian faith is one represented especially by St. Augustine. He had belonged to the Manichaeans[83] for ten years, and then, as a Christian, he turned against them in writings that are in large part polemical. But there are theologians who point out that some figures in Manichaean thought nevertheless influenced Augustine's theology and thus also had an impact on early Christianity. One consequence was, for example, the denigration of the body and sexuality in favor of the spirit. The contrast between flesh and spirit was narrowed to the realm of sexuality, and thus its real sense was lost. The consequences were rather dramatic. We hear an echo, for example, in Nietzsche's famous saying: "Christianity gave Eros poison to drink; he did not die of it, certainly, but degenerated to Vice."[84] Against this background, don't we need to get back to our roots and ask: What did Jesus and Paul really mean when they spoke of flesh and spirit?*

### Anselm Grün

Of course! For Christianity is, after all, the incarnation, the spirit's becoming flesh. Unfortunately, for a long time, throughout history, we have regarded the body as negative and sexuality as a danger instead of as vitality, creativity, strength, and a longing for union. Basically there is a good deal of mistrust here, and a new view of things is important. To be fair, however, we should also say that there is a mistrust of sexuality in Hinduism and Buddhism too—apart from the small branch of Tantrism. It appears that in all cultures and religions sexuality is seen as something ambivalent because it cannot be controlled. But it is important nowadays to approach sexuality positively and to find good ways of working with it—not in a spirit of negation or prohibition.

### David Steindl-Rast

I think it is very important not to confuse flesh with the body and spirit with intellect. We have to look at how skepticism about the "flesh," Greek *sarx*, arose historically, because then we can better understand what is meant. In the Near East the climate, as we know, is rather warm. When animals are slaughtered, the parts have to be processed pretty quickly. The ancients did not have refrigerators as we do today. In that hot climatic zone flesh spoiled and rotted quite rapidly. Hence flesh served very well as an image that was easy to understand. Flesh stands for what is vulnerable, easily spoiled, mortal.

Spirit, in turn, originally meant "breath" and represents vitality. As long as a being is breathing, it is alive. As long as flesh breathes, it does not decay. Only when the breath fails does it die and rot.

So if we keep in mind these images of flesh and breath we can see that this is about mortality and vitality. And the Christian doctrine of the incarnation celebrates that everything mortal is renewed by God's breath of life. God's vitality saturates all that is mortal.

### Anselm Grün

The passage in Paul about the "body as the temple of the Holy Spirit" (1 Cor 6:19) witnesses to that too. It is drawn from our experience. The human being radiates from her body. When we look at a person we experience the spirit in the body. Someone who has no relationship with her body cannot radiate anything. Only when soul and spirit stream through the body can we experience them. The spirit alone we cannot experience.

*In light of this corrupted history, do we need new ways today to reconcile body and spirit? That seems to me to be a reason why the physical forms of meditation from the East are attracting so many people here in the West. Be it yoga or Zen—here we can sense that the spirit is set right by means of bodily exercise and meditation. Here the connection can be felt.*

### David Steindl-Rast

Many are afraid of it because they think this is introducing something foreign. But the whole history of the Christian tradition witnesses that again and again, something good is drawn from outside. That is certainly nothing new.

### Anselm Grün

Meditation has been practiced in Christianity since the third century. Christians did not invent it; it is a great and ancient strand. Mantric prayer exists everywhere. The monks "baptized" it, you might say. Praying with the body and with physical action is also very important in Christianity. Since the Enlightenment we have totally neglected the body. When I pray with my whole body I am much more intensely present than when I only pray in my head. The head is always restless. The body gathers the spirit together. Yoga, after all, is also about binding.[85] The spirit is bound when I carry out certain actions.

There are such forms of meditation in Christianity also: one is sitting, the other is pilgrimage. The latter is also a bodily meditation that is now being rediscovered. Actions such as the Easter dance were an important form of expression in the Middle Ages. The sign of the cross and genuflection are little acts. It is also about experiencing oneself.

In the 1970s I was often with Karlfried Graf Dürckheim. He taught us about the body again in a very new way: I don't *have* a body; I *am* my body. Prayer happens in the body. For Dürckheim the body is a barometer that shows how things are with me. But the body is also an instrument of transformation, for when I sit down differently or stand firmly grounded, my inner attitude is also altered.

# Time for Gratitude, or:

## *Why Every Moment Is a Gift*

*Brother David, I learned something very important from you that I understood this way: Religious ideas, faith statements, and revealed religions are secondary in comparison to the primary existential ability to experience that is open to all people of all cultures and at all times. In short: before there is religion, first of all there is the experience of being. That means the opportunity is constantly offered me in every instant to begin something in life for myself. So my whole life becomes an opportunity to respond to this being that has been given me, to shape myself and my world creatively and hopefully to leave it a better place for my children and grandchildren. This experience of being is at the same time the source of gratitude and joy. And it is the beginning of original faith. Would you clarify this connection between gratitude, joy, and faith somewhat more precisely?*

### David Steindl-Rast

I am happy to talk about a life of gratitude. It is not only the heart of my own spirituality but also an attitude on which the survival of humanity could depend. Gratitude is connected to faith because it springs to life out of primal trust, that is, the primeval faith of the human being. Trusting in life is expressed when I gratefully make something of the opportunity life offers me in the given moment.

The connection between joy and gratitude is a fact of experience. We all know people who have everything they need to be happy and still are miserable, because they envy others, or want something different, or want more of the same, and so on. But we also know people who have very little or have to fight their way through life with great difficulty and yet they radiate joy. They don't have any luck, but they have joy—even in unhappiness.

If we look carefully at the difference between the miserable and those who enjoy life we see that it is gratitude. The unhappy rich are unhappy because they are not grateful for what they have. The happy poor are joyful in their misfortune because, in spite of everything, they are thankful. Gratitude is the key to joy, and joy is the happiness that does not depend on whether something makes us happy or not.

We can distinguish two steps on the path to this joy. We only have to remember how it feels when gratitude rises in us. An image may help us here: at the first step we are like a vessel that is slowly being filled. It rains, and the rain barrels fill up. When gratitude rises in our hearts it first happens in silence, but suddenly my heart runs over; the overflowing water gleams in the sunlight and pours out—then maybe I sing in the shower . . .

That is already the second step: giving thanks. So these are two things that belong together: gratitude and giving thanks. It is in giving thanks that our joy really shines.

But it doesn't often come to that in our consumer society. Just before our heart is about to overflow, we see an ad that tells us: "There is something better available," or "Your neighbor has a much newer model." Then we make our vessel bigger and bigger so that the water can never overflow. And yet it is only in the overflowing that our joy shines out. By contrast, when we visit countries where the people only have tiny vessels we are amazed that such poor people shine with joy. They only need a little to make their hearts overflow. But we can learn from that. We can make our own vessels a little smaller and so make our joy greater. It is not quantity of possessions that brings forth joy but the quality of a grateful life.

*I think it is important that what you are talking about is a phenomenological experience available to everyone, and not just a positive way of thinking, because it would be possible to see it very superficially in the sense of: "No negative thinking! Think positively! If you think positively, positive things will happen to you!" But those are simply psycho-tricks that promise something that does not match reality. What you have said touches something much deeper, and it interests me. What can we be grateful for? Where does that begin?*

### David Steindl-Rast

Gratitude always begins where two things come together: we have to receive something that matters to us, and it must be given to us as a free gift. When those two conditions coincide, gratitude rises spontaneously in the heart of every person.

The crucial step from this experience to a grateful life is in becoming aware that the most precious of all possible gifts is the given moment. If this moment were not given to us, there would be nothing else. The Now is the greatest gift, and it is pure gift. You can't buy a single instant with all the money and gold in the world. We see that when we are at death's door. Therefore it is helpful to keep death always before our eyes, as St. Benedict advises. Now, in this moment, and now, in the next moment, the greatest gift falls into my lap: the Now with all the opportunities it offers me.

**Anselm Grün**

I read your book[86] on gratitude with great pleasure, and it gave me a new idea: the word "thank" comes from "think." The one who thinks rightly is also grateful. Ungrateful people are unpleasant; you can never satisfy them. It is not a matter of course that we think and talk, even that we exist at all. Thinking means not only rational thought but also perception. The one who perceives the gift of the moment is grateful.

**David Steindl-Rast**

There are two extremes. One is not thinking at all and just living through the day. The other extreme is always thinking too much and inquiring skeptically into everything and being constantly suspicious that there is some kind of decoy that is going to lead one into a trap. So we somehow have to find a middle path in our thinking if it is going to lead to thanking and so to joy.

*How is it possible to be thankful when misfortune comes my way, when I think of the suffering and multiple injustices in this world, the exploitation, lies, corruption, and violence? How can I be grateful in the face of all that?*

### Anselm Grün

First, we don't have to be grateful all the time. When suffering comes, I am not grateful—that would be too heroic a gesture. In the midst of suffering I experience pain. But I can still remember that I have not only experienced suffering and that I am not only in pain. I may have people who stand by me so that I am not left alone, so that I am still alive. In the midst of suffering I will find something for which I can be grateful. It is like a handle to hold on to, so that I don't sink utterly into misery. Otherwise I would just be hanging there.

*Now I can say: good, as long as it is only about my private suffering, I agree, Father Anselm. But you have to admit: violence, hunger, corruption, exploitation, epidemics, lies, and betrayal—I am outraged by them! Surely I can't make my peace with them?*

### Anselm Grün

Of course I can't react to those with gratitude. Other attitudes are important here . . .

### David Steindl-Rast

Personally, I see gratitude as the fundamental attitude here as well. Naturally—here I agree with you—I don't believe you can be grateful for everything. There are a great many things for which we can't be grateful. You have listed some of them. But: in every situation we can be grateful because every moment gives us opportunity. The key word here is opportunity. You really said the same thing in different words. Even sickness and suffering often give us the opportunity to grow, or we learn something from them. Likewise, the situations of exploitation, war, and corruption give us the opportunity to protest and oppose them. Even an injustice that falls upon oneself or a colleague at work gives one the opportunity to act through the trade union or, if there is none, in person, to engage on behalf of justice and truth—right up to the cross, like Jesus. Doing something with the opportunities that are offered to us: for me that is the most important way to exercise gratitude. I concede that sometimes it can be very hard.

*I want to make this matter of gratitude even more complicated: Suppose that, materially speaking, things are going well for me. I can be grateful for that. But my materially good life may be a consequence of the fact that the relatively cheap goods that support my well-being were produced by people struggling with unjust working conditions and unfair pay. I can easily buy these material things because there are businesses that deplete the natural environment, and because they have the power to exploit their workers to the utmost.*

*Today, if I were to get on an airplane and fly to the Caribbean, I could be grateful that I can afford it and it is surely very beautiful there. But with my overseas flight I, like many others, would create a considerable quantity of greenhouse gases. Taken together, as we all know, they are contributing to a dangerous change in the climate. That change is already hitting the poorest of the poor to the worst degree. It leads to extreme natural events: droughts, floods, and in their wake to new poverty, hunger, and need. The poor have no other choice but to seek their fortune somewhere else. They gather on the coast of North Africa and board overloaded boats and barges and risk their lives in their desperate attempts to reach Europe. The whole scenario is being repeated in other forms in Latin America. Because of the massive inequality and the lack of opportunities for work and education, thousands of migrants are trying to cross the Mexican desert and enter the United States. They have already suffered enormously from the exploitation and violence of the "coyotes," and they can be happy if they are not murdered or do not die of thirst in the desert. The future that awaits them in the United States may be anything but rosy, even if they don't land in a holding camp as soon as they cross the border.*

*When I think of all that I no longer feel grateful for my material prosperity, because I sense that I share responsibility for the system that produces such scandalous conditions. So once more, briefly: How can I be grateful for superfluity when others pay the cost?*

## David Steindl-Rast

I show my gratitude by first pausing for a moment and taking a very sober look at the situation, as you have done. Then it becomes clear to me that I have to show myself grateful for the fact that I even *see* these grievances, by doing something to change the situation. A lot of people live like sleepwalkers; they aren't even aware of these bad situations. But we know, for example, that the coming global crisis will be not about oil but about water. It is well known that meat production uses enormous quantities of water. A pound of meat on my plate took as much water to produce as an ordinary person uses to shower in a whole year. Knowing that, I can, for example, deliberately eat less meat or go without any meat produced in mass-farming operations. I don't have to become a vegetarian overnight, but I could eat only a third as much meat as before or eat it only once a week.

That is one example of how each individual can make a small but quite concrete difference. But there are thousands of other possibilities, ways I can correct the injustice that has helped bring me the things for which I am grateful. The poor person who is exploited or has to flee because he has no water and too little to eat cannot do anything. I want to show my gratitude for the fact that I am in a situation in which I am given the opportunity to do something.

### Anselm Grün

There can be no doubt that the unjust situations you have described do exist, but, thanks be to God, a change in awareness is also happening. I wrote a book with the then-head of Puma, Jochen Zeitz.[87] Today no company in our country can any longer afford to sell soccer balls made by child labor. No one will buy them. There has been a shift in buyers' attitudes. In other matters things have not progressed so far. As far as food is concerned, we are not as advanced in Germany as they are in Austria and Switzerland, where more attention is being paid to these things. But a change in our thinking is happening. There is also gratitude that we no longer support unjust methods of production. After the catastrophic fires in the textile factories in Bangladesh, with hundreds of dead, the image of the providers of our fashionable labels has been so damaged that they can no longer afford to produce under such humanly degrading conditions. Civil society will not tolerate it.[88] The media have also discovered this subject of ethical responsibility for production and consumption. In a little while such things will no longer be possible.

**David Steindl-Rast**

This change in attitudes you speak of is indeed one of the major reasons for gratitude in our world, and at the same time it is being evoked by gratitude. For there is no awareness without reflection. Otherwise we are simply drawn into the flow of things. Close observation is necessary; the situation has to be analyzed. And change in attitude requires action. Clear knowledge has to lead to corresponding acts. But then we are back at the three-step process: "stop, look, go." Through that three-step movement we bring into being the innermost essence of gratitude.

*Brother David, you are building a network in Europe, the United States, Latin America, and China that is called "gratefulness.org" or "living gratefully."[89] It is a network of people from different countries and cultures who gather around the theme of gratitude, who want to live gratefully and give a spiritually engaged answer to suffering and injustice in our world. What are your hopes for that network? What could it bring about in our world? And: is it a network that also links religions together?*

**David Steindl-Rast**

The crucial step that we are taking in our projects is being awake. We are becoming aware that we have to educate people—especially our children—in gratitude. There are already schools, and projects in schools, that are built entirely on the basis of gratitude. For example, the Lutheran school directed by Margret Rasfeld in central Berlin is oriented to this principle and builds up gratitude both in the organization of the school and the structure of the daily program of instruction and also in the content of that instruction. This awareness that gratitude is revolutionary for our culture, and the fact that this awareness is now being introduced into education, gives me great hope.

*What is revolutionary about gratitude? Or: what changes if I live gratefully?*

### David Steindl-Rast

As I said: our dominant culture is marked by anxiety and fear. From that come violent behavior and dishonest competition, greed, and exploitation. Grateful living, in the first place, makes one fearless. It grows out of trust that everything that seems threatening to us brings with it an opportunity that gives us life. If we are grateful for these opportunities we no longer need to fear. The result of this fearlessness is then a peaceful spirit, respectful cooperation, and sharing. If we look only at these three fruits of gratitude—nonviolence, cooperation, and sharing—that is already something revolutionary in our world. If just one of them were to prevail, we would have a very different world. It is not hard to imagine how glorious a world in which people live together in gratitude might look. That is the world we desire.

*Father Anselm, would you say that religion, if traced to its core, is really a practice of gratitude?*

### Anselm Grün

Absolutely. The center of the Christian religion is the Eucharist, which means thanksgiving. In Greek, *eucharistein* means "give thanks." The liturgy is a giving thanks to God for what God has done for us. Every religion originates in gratitude for God's gift.

Of course, there are some religions that place more emphasis on fear of the negative, but the positive side of all religions is gratitude. We find this in Islam—gratitude for what God has given—and in Hinduism and Buddhism there is gratitude for being. It also exists in Christianity. In that sense it is an essential religious attitude to be grateful not only to other people but also to God for life, Nature, beauty, every moment of existence. That is a conscious life. The grateful person does not exploit and let things be. I take care of a gift; I do not throw it away.

### David Steindl-Rast

Yes, you are right: gratitude is an essential religious attitude—maybe the most essential. There is no religious or spiritual tradition in the world that does not say explicitly that gratitude is central to what it preaches and tries to practice. But gratitude goes beyond that: Even atheists and agnostics often say, "I am not religious and don't want anything to do with churches and spirituality. Living gratefully: that is my spirituality." So gratitude links all people together. It is an attitude in which a wholly new consciousness of community could join human beings together.

# Mysticism, Resistance, and Participation, or:

## What Is the Christian's Focus?

*Francis of Assisi[90] said to his assembled brothers and friends: We have been called to heal wounds, to unite what has fallen apart, and to bring home those who have lost their way. Pope Francis also speaks of the church's vocation to stand on the side of the poor and marginalized, of the victims of this wounded world.[91] To what degree must we make a reality of this core message of Christianity?*

### Anselm Grün

Pope Francis has restored an essential message of the Gospel to its place at the center. We see in many churches how money and power can be temptations. The church has to deliberately engage on behalf of the poor and those who are regarded as nothing in society. That is the spirit of Jesus. That is what St. Francis preached and lived, and many others as well. The "seven works of mercy"[92] used to be an important form of spirituality in the church. Despite all the deviations, we can say that if the church did not exist, our society would be essentially colder. But of course it is important to become aware, over and over again, of the real message of the Gospel because the danger of striving only for external power is also present in the church.

*Pope Francis also is not afraid of using some very harsh compari-*
*sons. He has called our capitalist economy an "economy that kills."[93]*
*He has set a new tone as he makes it clear how urgently we need*
*change, because today the fate of our planet is at stake, and this pope*
*seems to have grasped that.*

### David Steindl-Rast

We may call what the pope is aiming at a genuine re-
newal. We have spoken of how every tradition needs to
renew itself from the source. For the Christian tradition the
source is Jesus Christ. Jesus said nothing about orthodoxy,
but he had a lot to say about mercy. In recent decades the
church has concentrated much more on orthodoxy than
on mercy. Now, finally, Pope Francis is putting the main
emphasis on mercy. And that is what Jesus would probably
do today.

### Anselm Grün

Of course, the pope has not proclaimed a new economic
order. He can't do that. We have seen that Communism
does not bring us to the goal. Pure capitalism is also deadly.
It is true that Christian social teaching developed a social
market economics, but in the last thirty years it has been
badly disfigured.

*Besides, that approach lacks the ecological element. It must at least*
*be an eco-social model at its core.*

### Anselm Grün

Clearly. I speak now and then on values in the economy. By values I mean valuing creation and humanity or the Christian values of faith, hope, and love. At such times I encounter many people who are open to those values. I know businesses that genuinely try to live a Christian culture. I once held a talk at a firm where no one was ever fired. When times are bad for the company, the head of the firm is the first to go without his salary. That is a sign. The head aims at solidarity. There are various models. Sometimes when I give talks at companies I am accused of furnishing the business with an alibi. But I do it in the hope that those who are responsible there may also change their way of thinking. If those who are responsible are not greedy but instead pay attention to values, that is also a sign of hope that this world may be changing.

### David Steindl-Rast

A model suggested by Pope Leo XIII[94] but unfortunately never realized, even in the church, was the principle of subsidiarity. That would change the power pyramid at a stroke into a network. That is the hope for our future. It is plausible that every decision should be made at the lowest level where it can be made.

Take a simple example: the Austrian state railways. How a train station should be furnished, what personnel will be needed, or who will clean the station, and so on, can be decided at the regional level; the central office in Vienna need not make the choices. But the schedule must, of course, be prepared at a higher level because it requires the synchronization of a whole network. The things that can only be decided at the higher level are the sole matters that ought to be decided there.

If we were really to implement that in the church we would have a very different situation. Now most things come from above downward, but we urgently need to activate the movement from below upward.

# Speaking about Experiences, or:

## Does Faith Unite or Separate?

*In the history of the world's religions, there has been centuries-long competition, and often bloody conflict, both within the religions and between them. At present we can observe an example of it in Islamic jihadism. This happened, and happens, in the name of truth and in the name of God, but this religious conflict takes place on the basis of dualistic standpoints and totalitarian claims to truth and absoluteness. So: a religion is the true one and, therefore, the others are false and in error. One must either convince the others and convert them to one's own truth or, if that is not possible, combat or even destroy them. But when we dive deeper into the mystical traditions and the core experience of the religions we find a nondualistic way of thinking. That is a major contribution of the mystics. Could this mystical experience of faith open a way for us to learn to see one another anew and encounter one another more deeply? Then we could share the joy of faith and the cares of life; we could help one another and together make important contributions to the solution of urgent global problems. Is a new era of religious cooperation for justice, peace, and preservation of creation possible?*

## Anselm Grün

Mysticism is an important path to such, because it proceeds by way of experience and not through dogma. When I talk with others about my experiences I don't argue about

163

who is right; I am curious about the others' experience, and I respect it. The experiences of others can deepen my own. We discover in the process that this is about an experience of God and not about possessing the truth. God is truth. We are all only on the way toward truth.

If we take that seriously, the religions can cooperate well with one another. The future of the world depends very much on how the religions interact. Will they continue to be a source of wars, or will they instead be a source of reconciliation? Thanks be to God, in recent centuries there are some very positive signs. Christianity and Buddhism are good examples. There is dialogue with Hinduism. In the Middle Ages, Christianity and Islam were at one time coexisting in a good and productive way. Recently, in parts of Africa and the Near East that has become very problematic because of the attacks by extremists. In principle I think that the dialogue of the religions will decide the future of the world. But it must not be merely a dialogue about teachings; it must be about experience.

### David Steindl-Rast

I, too, think that our understanding of the experience of faith is decisive. It is faith that unites us. We always think that faith divides us. But it only divides us when we understand this or that teaching as faith. Rightly understood, religious faith does not consist in holding something to be true. Religious faith is trust—ultimately trust in God.

Trust in God—fearless trust in the unfathomable mystery of life—is something all human beings share. We only have to become aware of how we are bound together in faith.

This universal human primeval faith is expressed in the various traditions in quite different ways and is formulated in very different terms. But common to all us humans is trust in life, in the Mystery we point to with the word "God." Part of trusting in God is trusting in one another. Faith is ultimately what can join us all together in our innermost being.

# Thanks

## *Postlude* ex gratia

My first thanks are of course to Brother David and Father Anselm, who in spite of their overfilled calendars took time over a weekend to record their conversations in the abbey at Münsterschwarzach.

This book would probably not exist without an urging that came from abroad. Alberto Rizzo from Buenos Aires was the motivator, to whom sincere thanks are due at this point.

Special thanks to our editor, Marlene Fritsch, who graciously and persuasively worked with us to shape the book. Brother Linus Eibicht, head of Vier-Türme-Verlag, Dr. Matthias E. Gahr, Heike Rabeler, and several others at the publisher whose names I do not know took professional responsibility for seeing to it that this book would see the light at the beginning of the year 2015.

For tips and critical pointers I am very grateful to my friends, the graphic artist Clemens Schedler, the author Ilija Trojanow, my sister Veronika Kaup-Hasler, and, not least, my partner Silvia Tschugg. For their supporting ideas I want to thank Mirjam Luthe-Alves, Margaret Wakeley, and Brigitte Kwizda-Gredler of the network "Living Gratefully."

And for the fact that we were able together to bring to life such a beautiful and helpful project I offer my personal thanks to the Source of all life. That I can call that source by name, because it sustains me through life and death, is for me and has been all my life the source of a deeply felt happiness and life-giving joy.

Johannes Kaup
Vienna
November 2014

# Notes

[1] Friedrich Nietzsche (1844–1900), German philologist and philosopher. The quoted religious aphorism, no. 125, can be found under the subtitle "The Madman," in book 3 of *The Gay Science*, trans. Walter Kaufmann from the 2nd ed. (1887) of *Die fröhliche Wissenschaft* (New York: Random House, 1974), 181.

[2] Augustine of Hippo (354–430), philosopher, theologian, and bishop, was one of the four Latin fathers. His autobiography, *Confessiones*, written in 397, is his best-known work.

[3] Johann Wolfgang von Goethe (1749–1832), one of the most important German poets, was, together with Friedrich Schiller, the most significant representative of Weimar classicism.

[4] Plato (428–348 BCE) is regarded as one of the most influential ancient philosophers; his thinking has decisively influenced Western thought. He was a student of Socrates and the teacher of Aristotle.

[5] Simone Weil (1909–1943) was a French philosopher and mystic.

[6] Fyodor Mikhailovich Dostoevsky (1821–1881) was one of the most important Russian authors. Among his best-known works are *The Brothers Karamazov* and *Crime and Punishment*.

[7] Philip Grundlehner, *The Poetry of Friedrich Nietzsche* (New York: Oxford University Press, 1986), 26. Quoted in Bruce Ellis Benson, *Pious Nietzsche: Decadence and Dionysian Faith* (Bloomington, IN: Indiana University Press, 2008), 200–201.

[8] The concept of the "higher man" occurs in *Thus Spoke Zarathustra* (1883–1885).

[9] Bernard of Clairvaux (1090–1153), Doctor of the Church, mystic, and preacher of the Second Crusade, as abbot of Clairvaux spread the Cistercian order throughout Europe.

[10] Ludwig van Beethoven (1770–1824), Ninth Symphony in D-minor, Opus 125.

[11] Viktor Frankl (1905–1997), Austrian neurologist and psychiatrist, originated logotherapy and existential analysis. In *Man's Search for Meaning*, trans. Ilse Lasch (Boston: Beacon Press, 1992), he describes his experiences in German concentration camps.

[12] The Swiss psychiatrist and psychotherapist Daniel Hell (b. 1944) heads the Specialized Center for Depression and Anxiety at the private clinic of Hohenegg in Meilen, near Zürich.

[13] Johannes Tauler (1300–1361) was a Dominican friar, preacher, and mystic. He, together with Meister Eckhart and Heinrich Seuse, are counted as the three most important representatives of late medieval German Dominican spirituality.

[14] Ursula Nuber, *Die Egoismus-Falle. Warum Selbstverwirklichung so oft einsam macht* [The egoism trap: Why self-realization so often makes us lonely] (Zürich: Kreuz, 1993).

[15] Helen Keller (1880–1968) was an American author. She was both blind and deaf. She describes her experiences in, among other works, *The Story of My Life* (Garden City, NY: Doubleday, 1954).

[16] Martin Buber (1878–1965) was an Austrian-Israeli religious philosopher. He describes his dialogical approach in his most important work, *I and Thou* (New York: Scribner, 1958).

[17] Ferdinand Ebner (1882–1931) was an Austrian philosopher who is numbered with Martin Buber among the most important exponents of dialogical thought. His book is *Das Wort und die geistigen Realitäten. Pneumatologische Fragmente* [The word and spiritual realities: Pneumatological fragments] (Vienna: Lit, 2009).

[18] Henri Jozef Machiel Nouwen (1932–1996) was a Roman Catholic priest, psychologist, and spiritual writer from the Netherlands, the author of numerous works, including *The Genessee Diary: Report from a Trappist Monastery* (Garden City, NY: Doubleday, 1976).

[19] Marianne Gronemeyer, *Das Leben als letzte Gelegenheit. Sicherheitsbedürfnisse und Zeitknappheit* [Life as the last opportunity. Needs for security and shortness of time] (Darmstadt: Wissenschaftliche Buchgesellschaft, 2008).

[20] On this see Ilija Trojanow's essay, *Der überflüssige Mensch. Unruhe bewahren* [The superfluous human: Maintaining unrest] (Vienna: Residenz, 2013).

[21] Peter Sloterdijk, *You Must Change Your Life: On Anthropotechnics* (Cambridge, UK, and Malden, MA: Polity, 2013).

[22] Martin Heidegger, *Being and Time*, trans. Joan Stambaugh (Albany: SUNY Press, 2010). Heidegger contrasts "mineness" and the "they" and seeks the possibility of an authentic life, the real "being one's-self."

[23] Albert Görres (1918–1996), German psychoanalyst and psychotherapist, author of numerous books, including *Kennt die Religion den Menschen? Erfahrungen zwischen Psychologie und Glauben* [Does religion know humans? Experiences between psychology and faith] (Munich: Piper, 1983).

[24] Max Horkheimer (1895–1973), *Die Sehnsucht nach dem ganz Anderen—Ein Interview mit Kommentar von Helmut Gumnior* [The longing for the Wholly Other: An interview, with commentary, by Helmut Gumnior] (Hamburg: Furche, 1970).

[25] Krister Stendahl (1921–2008) was a Swedish Lutheran theologian, professor of New Testament at Harvard Divinity School, an expert on Paul, and from 1984 to 1988 the bishop of Stockholm.

[26] Karl Rahner (1904–1984) was one of the most important Catholic theologians of the twentieth century and a *peritus* at Vatican II. His work included numerous books and articles, including *On the Theology of Death*, QD 2 (New York: Herder and Herder, 1961).

[27] Shunryū Suzuki (1905–1971) was a Japanese Sōtō-Zen Master. Suzuki made Zen popular in the United States and Germany, in part through his book, *Zen Mind, Beginner's Mind*, ed. Trudy Dixon (New York: Walker/Weatherhill, 1970).

[28] The difference between being and existence is called the "ontological difference" or "ontic-ontological difference" in philosophy. The distinction stems from the philosophy of Martin Heidegger. In his *Being and Time*, being is the horizon of understanding on the basis of which this-worldly existence encounters us. Being is the precondition for all existence. But the being of the existent is usually forgotten (see also "forgetfulness of being"). Thus, for example, no emphasis is placed on the fact that for a given thing to exist there must be a given and a giver.

[29] "Negative theology" is a philosophical way of thinking about God or the One that is derived from Platonism. It regards all positive expressions about God (God is described according to particular characteristics, for example, God is good/true/just, etc.) as inadequate. The reason given is that in such cases human experiences are being

transferred to God, but in principle they cannot correspond to God's absolute transcendence. Only negative statements can be regarded as true (for example, God is not like . . .). "Negative" should not be understood as an expression of value.

[30] Heinrich Böll (1917–1985) was a German author who received the Nobel Prize for Literature in 1972. He was active, among other things, in resistance to National Socialism and in human rights concerns in Latin America. Böll also took a critical stance toward the Catholic Church and formally left it in 1976 without, as he said, having "fallen away from the faith."

[31] See Karl Rahner, *Foundations of Christian Faith: An Introduction to the Idea of Christianity* (New York: Seabury, 1978).

[32] Johann Baptist Metz (b. 1928) was regarded as the father of the "new" political theology (the "old" political theology goes back to Carl Schmitt). Metz was the theological prophet of "compassion." On this see his *Memoria Passionis: Ein provozierendes Gedächtnis in pluraler Gesellschaft* [*Memoria Passionis*: A provocative memory in pluralist society] (Freiburg: Herder, 2006).

[33] Richard Baker Roshi (b. 1936) is an American Zen teacher in the tradition of Dongshan (9th c.) and Shunryū Suzuki Roshi. Baker Roshi became a Dharma follower of Suzuki Roshi in 1971 and since that time has been bringing Buddhist teaching to the West.

[34] Augustinus Karl Wucherer-Huldenfeld (b. 1929), *Philosophische Theologie im Umbruch* [Philosophical theology in upheaval], 2 vols. (Vienna: Böhlau, 2011). The third volume (II/2) was published by Böhlau in 2015; see also his *Befreiung und Gotteserkenntnis* [Liberation and the knowledge of God], ed. Karl Baier (Vienna: Böhlau, 2009).

[35] Hans Küng, *Global Responsibility: In Search of a New World Ethic*, trans. John Bowden (New York: Crossroad, 1991).

[36] Irenaeus of Lyons (135–202), church father, saint from Smyrna, and bishop of Lugdunum/Lyons. The writings of this systematic theologian gave direction to early Christianity and its development. The concept of the *regula fidei*, the "rule of faith," goes back to Irenaeus.

[37] *Hypostasis* means "basis," in a philosophical context "level of being" or "reality."

[38] The so-called Cappadocian fathers—Basil of Caesarea, Gregory of Nyssa, and Gregory Nazianzus—are important Doctors of the Church from the fourth century CE, all of them native to Cappadocia (today's

central Anatolia in Turkey). They contributed decisively to the victory of the doctrine of the Trinity in the "Arian controversy."

[39] Rainer Maria Rilke (1875–1926) was one of the most important poets of literary modernity. His best-known works include the three-volume *Book of Hours*, the *Duino Elegies,* and the *Sonnets to Orpheus.*

[40] Willigis Jäger (b. 1925) is a German Benedictine monk, a Zen master and mystic. In 2003, Jäger became director of the transconfessional meditation center Benediktushof in Holzkirchen. Together with Anselm Grün, he is the author of a book edited by Winfried Nonhoff, *Das Geheimnis jenseits aller Wege: Was uns eint, was uns trennt* [The mystery beyond all paths: What unites us, what separates us] 2nd ed. (Münsterschwarzach: Vier-Türme, 2014).

[41] Joseph von Eichendorff (1788–1857) was an important lyricist and author in the German romantic period.

[42] T. S. Eliot (1888–1965), *Four Quartets* (1935): "Burnt Norton," 1.

[43] Teresa of Ávila (1515–1582) was a Spanish mystic and Carmelite. She was elevated to the rank of Doctor of the Church and is honored as a saint in the Catholic Church.

[44] "Meister Eckhart," Eckhart von Hochheim (1260–1328) was one of the most prominent theologians, philosophers, and mystics of the late Middle Ages. One of the chief concerns of this Dominican friar was to spread a spiritual practice of life among the people. See also Meister Eckhart, *German Sermons & Treatises*, trans. Maurice O'C. Walshe, 2 vols. (London: Watkins, 1979–1981).

[45] This is more the case in German, where the words "to ask" and "to pray" are, respectively, "bitten" and "beten."—Trans.

[46] The reference is to "the glory of God is the human being fully alive; the life of the human being is the vision of God," a quotation from Irenaeus of Lyons, *Adversus Haereses* 4.20.7.

[47] Ebner, *Das Wort und die geistigen Realitäten.*

[48] Worth reading: Richard Rohr, *Contemplation in Action* (Albuquerque, NM: Center for Action and Contemplation, 2006).

[49] From Rainer Maria Rilke, *The Book of Hours*, trans. Annemarie S. Kidder (Evanston, IL: Northwestern University Press, 2001), 68, 55. Both passages occur within the first book, "The Book of the Monkish Life" (1899).

[50] Benedict of Nursia (480–547) founded the first Benedictine monastery in 529 on Monte Cassino in a former temple of Apollo.

[51] The Trappists are characterized by strict rules of silence and prayer apart from the world. They are an independent order that began in the seventeenth century as a reform branch of the Cistercians.

[52] The cellarer (from Latin *cellarium*, storeroom) was originally the steward in Benedictine houses; today the cellarer is the business manager of the abbey.

[53] The idea of the monk is derived from the Greek word *monachōs* ("alone," "sole").

[54] The three ways can be traced to Dionysius the Areopagite, the father of "negative theology" (see n28, above).

[55] The German verbs are "stellen" (to put or place) and "stehen-bleiben" (to stop).—Trans.

[56] In Buddhism the personal experience of enlightenment that recognizes the universal nature of Being is called *satori* (see also "Buddha nature" or "source").

[57] Evagrius Ponticus (345–399), Greek "Evagrios Pontikos," theologian and monk ("Desert Father"), mediator of monastic spirituality between the Orient and the Occident. Evagrius was the creator of the doctrine of the eight vices, a spiritual psychology he adopted from John Cassian and developed further.

[58] Peter Schellenbaum (b. 1939), Catholic theologian and psychoanalyst, author of many books, has been running an institute for education and therapy in Orselina, near Locarno, in Switzerland, since 1993.

[59] Gregory the Great (540–604), youngest of the four great Latin fathers, wrote the biography of St. Benedict of Nursia.

[60] Karlfried Graf Dürckheim (1896–1988) was a German psychotherapist and Zen teacher. Together with Maria Hippius, he introduced Initiatic Therapy.

[61] See, for example, the men's spiritual work of Richard Rohr (initiation rituals for men: https://cac.org/events/menaslearnerselders/mrop) and his book *Adam's Return: The Five Promises of Male Initiation* (New York: Crossroad, 2004).

[62] Eugen Drewermann (b. 1940), German theologian, psychoanalyst, and author. He is one of the best-known representatives of depth-psychology biblical exegesis and the author of many books. The reference here is to his earliest work, *Strukturen des Bösen* (*Structures of Evil*), which was his dissertation (1977).

[63] Thomas Aquinas (1225–1274) was the most important theologian and philosopher of medieval high scholasticism; he is one of the thirty-five Catholic Doctors of the Church and was also called "Doctor Angelicus." His principal work is the *Summa Theologiae*. He was canonized in 1323.

[64] *Privatio boni* means an absence of the good and signifies that evil has no substance of its own. It lives parasitically on the good. Thomas Aquinas offers the example of blindness, which exists because the light of the eyes is absent.

[65] Latin *peccatum originale*, primal sin, original sin. Augustine formulated the doctrine of original sin as the central pillar of Western Christianity. It is true that, despite original sin, human beings can choose the good, but only through the aid of God's grace. Because original sin is considered a permanent condition of deficiency, the need of human beings for redemption follows necessarily. This is made possible through Jesus Christ, who became human (incarnation), was crucified, and is risen. The apostle Paul speaks of Christ in this context as the "new Adam" (see Rom 5:12-21).

[66] In Buddhism, *dukkha* (suffering, from Sanskrit; literally "hard to bear") is regarded as one of the three characteristics of existence and the first of the Four Noble Truths.

[67] Paul Tillich (1886–1965) was a German-American Protestant systematic theologian and religious philosopher. After his emigration from Germany he taught at Harvard University and the University of Chicago. Tillich was one of the most influential theologians of the first half of the twentieth century, alongside Karl Rahner, Karl Barth, Rudolf Bultmann, and Dietrich Bonhoeffer.

[68] The reference is to the German *Einheitsübersetzung*, an ecumenical translation. The NRSV has "they are now justified by his grace as a gift, through the redemption that is in Christ Jesus, whom God put forward as a sacrifice of atonement by his blood, effective through faith" (Rom 3:24-25) but adds a note at "sacrifice of atonement": "Or *a place of atonement.*"

[69] John 1:29: Jesus is called the Lamb of God (Greek *amnōs tou theou*; Latin *agnus dei*) in the NT. In the Gospel of John, the Baptizer points to Jesus as the Lamb of God. It became an early Christian symbol for Jesus Christ. In addition, the "Agnus Dei" is a fixed part of the Roman Catholic liturgy of the Mass.

[70] The Greek concept of *logismoi* (plural of *logismos*) refers to passions, unconscious thoughts, spiritual images, or "seeds of passion."

[71] Johannes Cassianus (360–435) was a desert monk, abbot, and a theological writer. He listed as the principal vices intemperance, unchastity, avarice, wrath, lugubriousness, tedium, pride. Later these became the seven cardinal sins. The principal vices also play a role in his major work, *Collationes patrum*, which appeared in three volumes. See John Cassian, *Conferences*, ed. Colm Luibheid, Classics of Western Spirituality (Mahwah, NJ: Paulist Press, 1985).

[72] In philosophy, *apatheia* is seen as a positive calmness and equanimity and so as something worth striving for. The use of the term in medicine is completely different: there apathy is understood as listlessness, a symptom of illness.

[73] Poimēn the Great (340–450), famed Desert Father of late antiquity, lived in an Egyptian monastery. He is honored as a saint in all the Orthodox churches and in the Catholic Church as well.

[74] See Anselm Grün, *Heaven Begins Within You: Wisdom from the Desert Fathers* (New York: Crossroad, 2000).

[75] Wolfgang Schmidbauer (b. 1941) is a German psychoanalyst and author. His works include *Alles oder Nichts. Über die Destruktivität von Idealen* [All or nothing: On the destructiveness of ideals] (Hamburg: Rowohlt, 1987); *Das Helfersyndrom. Über Hilfe für Helfer* [The helper syndrome: Help for helpers] (Hamburg: Rowohlt Taschenbuchverlag, 2007).

[76] In slang it means "bonkers," crazy, being possessed by fixed (insane) ideas.

[77] "Structures of sin" is a concept from the 1987 encyclical *Sollicitudo rei socialis* ("The Social Concern of the Church"). John Paul II writes there: "Moreover, one must denounce the existence of economic, financial and social mechanisms which, although they are manipulated by people, often function almost automatically, thus accentuating the situation of wealth for some and poverty for the rest. These mechanisms, which are maneuvered directly or indirectly by the more developed countries, by their very functioning favor the interests of the people manipulating them and in the end they suffocate or condition the economies of the less developed countries."

[78] The "multiplication of the loaves" is found in the New Testament at John 6:2-14; Luke 9:11-17; Mark 6:33-46; and Matt 14:13-23.

[79] "Suffering is the bedrock of atheism" is a quotation from the philosopher Ludwig Feuerbach (1804–1872) that was taken up by the author Georg Büchner (1813–1837): "Theodicy is the rock of atheism."

[80] James Fowler, *Stages of Faith: The Psychology of Human Development and the Quest for Meaning* (San Francisco: Harper & Row, 1981).

[81] Jean Piaget (1896–1980) was a Swiss developmental psychologist. See his book, *The Origins of Intelligence in Children*, trans. Margaret Cook (New York: International Universities Press, 1952).

[82] Leonard Cohen, "Anthem," lyrics at https://www.google.com/?gws_rd=ssl#q=leonard+cohen+anthem+lyrics.

[83] Manichaeanism is a Gnostic form of belief traced to the Persian Mani. Manichaeanism is strongly dualistic. Its adherents are supposed to achieve redemption through asceticism and continued striving for purity.

[84] In *Beyond Good and Evil*.

[85] Well worth reading in this connection are the works of the history of religions scholar Karl Baier, who teaches at the University of Vienna: *Yoga auf dem Weg nach Westen. Beiträge zur Rezeptionsgeschichte* [Yoga on its way to the West: Contributions to the history of reception] (Würzburg: Königshausen & Neumann, 1998); *Meditation und Moderne* [Meditation and modernity], 2 vols. (Würzburg: Königshausen & Neumann, 2009).

[86] David Steindl-Rast, *Gratefulness, the Heart of Prayer: An Approach to Life in Fullness* (Mahwah, NJ: Paulist Press, 1984).

[87] Anselm Grün and Jochen Zeitz, *The Manager and the Monk: A Discourse on Prayer, Profit, and Principles*, trans. Susan Thorne (San Francisco: Jossey-Bass, 2013).

[88] One example is the international Clean Clothes Campaign: http://www.cleanclothes.org.

[89] Website: http://www.gratefulness.org.

[90] Francis of Assisi (1181–1226) was born Giovanni Battista Bernadone. Francis, canonized in 1228, lived according to the model set by Jesus in the gospels, in simplicity and humility. His radically simple way of life and loving care for the poor and sick rapidly drew like-minded people to him. From these arose the community of the Friars Minor (Franciscans), as well as the Poor Clares. The Argentine cardinal of Buenos Aires, Jorge Mario Bergoglio, SJ, chosen pope in

2013, was the first pope in history to take the name Francis; thus he set up a symbol of repentance for the Catholic Church.

⁹¹ See, among others, Pope Francis's first apostolic exhortation, *Evangelii Gaudium* ("The Joy of the Gospel") of November 24, 2013, with its subtitle, "On the Proclamation of the Gospel in Today's World." Available at http://w2.vatican.va/content/francesco/en/apost _exhortations/documents/papa-francesco_esortazione-ap_20131124 _evangelii-gaudium.html.

⁹² The seven works of mercy are listed in Matthew's gospel (Matt 25:31-46): feeding the hungry, giving drink to the thirsty, sheltering strangers, clothing the naked, caring for the sick, visiting prisoners, and burying the dead.

⁹³ In *Evangelii Gaudium*, Pope Francis calls for a struggle against poverty (see esp. no. 202).

⁹⁴ Leo XIII (1810–1903) was called the "workers' pope" for his sensitivity to the social issues of his time. His most important encyclical on this subject was *Rerum Novarum* (1891).